A year without months

Charles Dodd White

WEST VIRGINIA UNIVERSITY PRESS
MORGANTOWN

Copyright © 2022 by Charles Dodd White
All rights reserved
First edition published 2022 by West Virginia University Press
Printed in the United States of America

ISBN 978-1-952271-52-6 (paperback) / 978-1-952271-53-3 (ebook)

Library of Congress Cataloging-in-Publication Data
Names: White, Charles Dodd, 1976– author.
Title: A year without months / Charles Dodd White.
Description: First edition. | Morgantown : West Virginia University Press,
    2022. | Series: In place
Identifiers: LCCN 2021053324 | ISBN 9781952271526 (paperback)
    | ISBN 9781952271533 (ebook)
Subjects: LCSH: White, Charles Dodd, 1976—Family. | Appalachian
    Region, Southern—Biography. | Rural life—Appalachian Region,
    Southern. | Suicide—Appalachian Region, Southern—Psychological
    aspects. | Masculinity—Appalachian Region, Southern—Psychological
    aspects. | Atlanta (Ga.)—Biography.
Classification: LCC F217.A65 W478 2022 | DDC 975—dc23
    /eng/20211108
LC record available at https://lccn.loc.gov/2021053324

Book and cover design by Than Saffel / WVU Press

Altered versions of these essays have appeared previously in the follow-
ing publications: "Groupings," *Rumpus*, September 2013; "Bethlehem
Bottoms," *Louisville Review*, Summer 2012; "Why I Don't Hunt
Anymore," *Bitter Southerner*, October 2019; "What We Gain in the
Hurt," in *Walk Till the Dogs Get Mean*, edited by Adrian Blevins and
Karen Salyer McElmurray (Ohio University Press, 2015)

IN PLACE

Jeremy Jones, Series Editor
Elena Passarello, Series Editor

American Vaudeville
Geoffrey Hilsabeck

This Way Back
Joanna Eleftheriou

The Painted Forest
Krista Eastman

Far Flung: Improvisations on National Parks, Driving to Russia, Not Marrying a Ranger, the Language of Heartbreak, and Other Natural Disasters
Cassandra Kircher

Lowest White Boy
Greg Bottoms

On Homesickness: A Plea
Jesse Donaldson

For
Ethan Tichenor White
(1997–2015)
and
Melanie White
(1945–2020)

Contents

———

Preface

—

It interests me how much we forget the way the change of seasons can affect us. The cooling of late autumn wakes up the world, makes it so particular and needed. Perception sharpens, as does the desire to move. I become more contained within my body, more alertly animal. I can detect details of a larger nature.

People dismiss conversations about weather as mere ritual, a way to fill blank space. But I also think the question of weather can be something more. When we talk about the weather with someone, we let the person know that we care about how they are faring, how well they're enduring what we all have to.

So I write this in the turn toward the colder season, and I sit in a stone house nearly eighty years old. I like that our home is made of rock, built by a different scale of time. The rooms are quiet except for the soft circulations of our pets. When our son died, we tried to fill the place with their life.

When you lose a child, time shuffles. It rejects coherence. You are left in a shock wave of permanently changed circumstances. You can immediately glimpse a kind of limitless horizon of grief, a landscape that stretches in all directions, reaching back as well as forward, so that memories, even the dearest of them, are compromised by pain. The parents of dead children reach for many metaphors to express this depth of hurt, but so many efforts to convey the experience fail because the loss is more complicated than a matter of intensity. The real disquiet that enters the mind of a stricken parent is the intimacy of the death. The event amputates, and the absence that remains takes up space in a way nothing else can. You feel how physically weak emotion can render you, how you can be fundamentally reduced.

Ethan took his own life at eighteen in October 2015, a day shy of Halloween. It wasn't a holiday that held any particular significance for me. My mind had been preoccupied that week by a medical concern with my wife, April, which later turned out to be something of no consequence, but at the time it burdened. When we got the all clear from the doctor, we drove home and opened a bottle of champagne. We drank, enjoyed our first fire of the season, and thought we had evaded something threatening and final.

Burning wood became my private ritual through the several weeks following his death. Sometimes in the company of some friend who had come to express condolences, but often just me, drunk on the flames as much as whatever liquor I had at hand. I watched the fire like it was a movie of something I was on the verge of understanding. In time, the fire pried out several memories of not only Ethan but also the other men in my family I'd lost in the same way, subtracted from this life by their own hands. An absurd trigonometry, I realized. Three men, the three closest in blood—my father, my uncle, and my son—all dead by suicide. I marvel at the sheer statistical improbability of that. What could it be? One in a million? A trillion? Still, somehow I have no desire to follow them. The riddle of that is as insoluble as anything I can imagine.

This question has always been foremost in my mind. Because of that, these essays are collected from over the past decade, though most have been written "as a piece" since Ethan's death. I wanted to show a larger family story, how we struggled with and succumbed to the elements that reach out and try to grab hold of the living. I hope their lives will find a place in your memory, so that who they were can be larger than my singular recollection. I hope too that what's written here may show that my surviving them was to a good purpose.

Groupings

—

GUNS FORMED me. They worked on my body, bruising it in all the right places. Recoil and report learned they couldn't scare me off. Each weapon wrote its own angry truth. Some boys take their licks after school, perhaps fending off bullies, perhaps bullying others. But I got my knocks from a Remington. The act of being hit and hitting back are two sides of the same conversation, and there are plenty of things to learn from what that kind of language has to say given enough time, attentiveness, and grit.

The men of my family, the distinct personalities who have made me who I am, were found parts jammed into rough agreement. My uncle was my substitute father. Why he took on that role, I've never been completely sure. Perhaps it was to have a captive pupil, someone to drag along to Civil War battlefield sites so he could teach the legacy of defeat. Or maybe it was simply to fill out his bachelor life, turn back middle-aged loneliness with the bonus of feeling like he was helping his sister. Those two rarely spared a kind word for each other, but I suppose both were getting something out of the arrangement, and there was never much argument about how I would spend my weekends. My father had never been around other than for a couple of half-hearted visitations, and when I was seven, a cousin told me that he'd died. At the time, I didn't think to ask what from.

So my uncle took on the business of raising me up. I adopted his habits, aped his mannerisms. His obsessions became mine. Few men in this life have enjoyed handling guns as much as he did. Evenings before the television were spent with disassembled Marlins, Brownings, and Smith and Wessons, both long guns and short. He showed me how to punch bores with wire brushes and then follow through with cleaning patches folded into the shape of soft diamonds. The way the guns gleamed afterward gave me a sense of something shared, something mutually accomplished.

And then there was the firing range. The practice of shooting and the need to belong to a proper idea of manhood were quickly soldered in me. A day spent on the firing line shooting at beer bottles on the empty right-of-way beneath a power line let me know something about myself, about how well I could accept the punishment of a rifle's kickback. That moment of composure and necessary self-mastery as I touched the tip of my finger to the trigger was everything. The reckless, urgent violence belonged to the bullet. The control was mine alone.

As I got older, I was brought along on hunts, made part of the deer camp. I worked hard, cleared brush by hand, carried salvage lumber, ripped down rotten deer stands. This earned my place and guaranteed I had a bunk and access to as many practice rounds as I needed. We hunted in the mornings and evenings, but the middle of the day was devoted to target practice.

I learned the geometry of aligning iron sights and scopes to the strike of the bullet on distant targets. I perfected my form, the consistency of execution. The rifle was held exactly the same during each shot—the angle of the sight to the eye, the tension in the grip, the meld of the cheek to the buttstock—so that the rounds appeared within a tolerable distance of one another on the target. These groupings, usually three shots, had to be close enough to one another to be covered with a quarter in order to take a worthwhile measurement. Then it was only a matter of a few clicks on the rear sight V-notch, and another round or two to confirm a cut of the bull's-eye.

I was patient in my apprenticeship. I liked gaining the confidence and readiness of excellent marksmanship. The crack and hard recoil of the rifle or pistol doing what it was meant to do split through everything else. The practice of putting rounds on target was pure definition.

When, as a teenager, I learned that my father had killed himself, I didn't feel grief. There was no center for emotion, no entry point for trauma. Life doesn't yield such psychic conveniences. It was only another story, a blur in the fog. But today, whenever I pick up a rifle and sight, I cannot help but think of my father. I cannot forget the shot he took, a shotgun in the mouth, leaving the simple matter that comprised his character on the bathroom tile. The fact of it grows larger as I grow older, as I near the age he was at the time of his death. One day I will be older than my father ever was. I often wonder what shade of wisdom I should have gained by that time.

WHEN MY uncle was a boy, he learned to disappoint his father, the same way his father had been a disappointment in turn, by the simple fact of being who he was. For starters, they bore the same name: William Virgil Dodd. My grandfather was a junior, my uncle the third. Though I only knew my grandfather the last seven years of his life, the old man made a strong impression on me. He was largely kind and patient, instructive, bearing himself like he knew I was paying close attention. Even in retirement, he worked hard, picking up odd jobs in the community, employing his natural handiness in small tasks, mostly in barter. Our family never lacked for seafood suppers because of the door repairs he did for a local restaurant. The deliverymen were hard on screen doors, apparently. He showed me how to tie a necktie and use a carpenter's square. He read Br'er Rabbit stories to me before we took afternoon naps together in the long Georgia afternoons.

But like most of the Dodd men, my grandpa was prone to bouts of drunkenness, crawling through the house on all fours and hollering, pained by the chemical madness afflicting his better reason. My grandmother tried to shelter me from his fits, but I saw more than the adults believed I did. I don't remember feeling frightened, only betrayed by the realization that he was the helplessly contradictory mess that real people always are.

Sometimes, when he was of a calmer turn, he brought me into his bedroom where we would eat canned ravioli and vienna sausages he kept in his louvered closet. He avoided my grandmother as much as he could, the best parts of their marriage broken long before by terrible fighting and resentment, and he kept this space as his own private larder. While we ate, he would tell me stories, often about hunts he had gone on, taking my uncle along with him. They would drive to the mountains of north Georgia in the fall, pitching great canvas tents under skies so cold they seemed on the verge of cracking. I would imagine deer bounding across ridgelines, bears tiptoeing through sleeping camps, their nostrils wide and hot. And then I would see my male kin moving out through this strange wilderness, rifles and scatterguns tilting from their shoulders as they went out into the woods together.

When my uncle told me many of these stories years later, they took on a different cast. He recalled many of the same events, but in his versions he was always alone, circumscribed. He spoke of "Daddy," but there was a distinct if fond sadness in his tone. There was no doubt that some profound break had occurred. My uncle was a mercurial and weak man, and his capacity to turn against those who had stood by him in the most difficult of times never failed to rob him of the kind of deep loyalty he desired. The few instances I remember of my uncle and grandfather together in the same room are colored with a kind of gloom and silence that spoke of some weight beyond my knowledge. Later, I would hear of drunken quarrels that devolved into fistfights and possibly weapons drawn, but I never learned the specifics of this discord. I still marvel at how dissimilar they were from each other, as much as I am now from them.

While my uncle was a veteran of Vietnam, my grandfather never served in the military, having been too old to be drafted during World War II. It's tempting to speculate on the tension this might have caused between them, but despite knowing how often the two could scrap like two cocks in a pit fight, I never remember my uncle being anything other than a grown-up little boy around his father. There was always something desperate in him, something frantic for approval, a desire to have his manhood confirmed. Even the military and a foreign war hadn't been enough to give him that.

The three of us made only one hunt together. It was in the early spring, turkey season, the spring before my grandfather would collapse from a stroke in the middle of the night, quietly dying while I slept down the hall. I was staying with him and my grandmother a lot then. He would take me into the back lot and show me how to shoot squirrels and check them for wolf worms before skinning the critters out.

He and I were working outside, mowing grass on his riding silver lawn mower when my uncle swung up the rutted drive in his Cadillac Eldorado, bouncing twice hard before kicking gravel across the grass in a sudden stop.

"Pack your gear," he said, half-breathless. "The woods are slap full of gobblers."

My grandfather threw the mower's shift into neutral and cut the engine.

"It's the right time of year for it, I guess," he said.

"I'm telling you, Daddy. You've never seen anything like it. I must have had half a dozen birds within range."

The old man glanced over his shoulder and squinted.

"That right? Where they at then?"

My uncle ignored this jab, telling us to hurry up. Pretty soon the prospect was too much for my grandfather to pass up. We went into the house, made a phone call to my mother to tell her we'd be out of touch overnight, equipped ourselves with camouflage, thermoses, box calls, shotguns, and shells. Within the hour, we were clearing commuter traffic, headed south for the promised land my uncle claimed to have discovered.

We got in late, too late to even step into the woods for any afternoon scouting. It was nearly twilight, and storm clouds were gathering low and hot. You could feel the menace of electric turbulence coming on. We hurried into the longhouse and dumped the Piggly Wiggly groceries on a mildewed card table. Just as we got settled, the sky simply opened, the rain falling straight down and heavy. It struck the tin roof like something it meant to crush.

After we'd eaten steaks off a hibachi grill with some mixed potatoes and onions, we moved out to the covered porch area, though it lacked anything in the way of flooring, and the water in the yard ran up under our boots so that we sloshed mud whenever we ventured a few steps. Lightning bleached everything. My uncle unscrewed the cap on a plastic traveler of Jim Beam. It passed back and forth between the two men while I listened to the language in their mouths turn to gum. I knew it was time to go to bed when they began cursing under their breath, eyes bright in the strobe.

There was a buried anger between them that terrified me, the same kind of rage and capacity to hate that lives in me as a grown man. It's easy to blame so much on event and circumstance, but I can't know what causes this darkness in my family, why we wreck our bodies and minds with alcohol and self-pity. Something burns in us. Dodd men hold up a mirror to one another by the very fact of our existence, and the similarities we see in one another expose this confusion, this lack. This was what I saw between my uncle and grandfather. They could not forgive each other for the things they had in common, just as they could never stop loving each other for the same reason. The woods and the hunt were their escape from a world that seemed increasingly foreign and indifferent to their deepest identity. They were trapped together finally by the same passion.

As a grown man, I suffer many of my uncle's and grandfather's fundamental incompleteness, but the fruits of my experience have borne themselves distant from their roots. Like them, I have managed my relationships with those I love poorly. I have seen how this has affected my own son. He has too often been a second thought in my life, deferred by abstractions that seemed so important at the time. I expect a toughness in him that he shouldn't have to take on as his own. Also, the dangerous loneliness and distorted suffering that drinking causes has been part of my failures as a human being. I have the same capacity for acrimony and bitterness my uncle and grandfather did. And I've seen what it is to fall short of my ideas of what a good man should be. There are fewer moments more profoundly desperate in a life than that. I hope it was the same for them. I want to believe that the ache of their deficit testified to the worthiness of what they were trying to become, but it's hard to be sure.

Perhaps that's where the greatest departure was. Even as a boy, I understood that I moved through the world differently. There was caution in my actions, weight in my hesitation. I find great importance in the well-balanced moment. There is beauty in comprehending the absolute complexity of a specific etch in time, irreversible and potent. These men never seemed to grasp that regret might numb them to what remained of their lives. They simply collided with each other, fiercely opposite wills playing out against mutual antagonism. The conflict itself was reflexive, mindless. The real violence between them was in its essential meaninglessness. They battered each other because it was a way to injure themselves, and that was ultimately the only way they knew to wait out death.

I am terrified of not only death but also emptiness. I want to find the hidden corrections that will make my life matter, wherever they may lie. I believe they can be found somewhere in the coolness of self-possession. I am still looking, still trying to catch my breath.

WHEN HE was eight, I took my son, Ethan, to a deer camp in Columbus, Georgia. The Chattahoochee River to the west is big and brown, a slow border with Alabama. The lease was one of many within a large tract of land exploited by the Mead paper company. The pine was all straight and tall, simple vertical strokes on the landscape. These trees, too, would likely be harvested in time, the thinned forest razed for cheap pulpwood. It was more a farm than a true hunting ground. Small particleboard cabins had been set up where the various hunt clubs held their leases; my uncle and his longtime hunting buddy, Charlie, had hauled down a small camper on wheels and built a longhouse around it, bolting the exterior walls and roof in place so that the entire structure could be disassembled and moved if the lease wasn't renewed the following season.

Ethan and I were up earlier than the others the next morning. I wanted to clear camp before my uncle and Charlie had time to wake up and slow us down with their coffee and cigarettes. I wanted to give my son a chance to have a better understanding of who I was and how the woods could be so important to a boy. He was quiet as we mounted the trail, but he often is, and he seemed good-natured about tramping out into the crisp predawn dark. That spoke well of him. He wanted to commit himself to the hunt without complaint. He wanted to be part of the same life I did.

By first light, we had settled into a ground blind, sitting only a few feet apart. We each passed the morning with a book, reading a few lines and pausing to scan the woods, watch the early fog rise. Ever since he was first able to read, Ethan has been able to immerse himself in books. He is studious and focused in a way I admire. I've always been hectic in my attention, putting down a book after a couple of minutes to think about what has passed under my eye. It's odd to recognize some quality in your child that in no sense belongs to you. There, in the enigma of individual character, might be the reason we really desire to have children. Not so much to guarantee a better future as to experiment with a different set of personalities, to see how the world might turn out under the guidance of hands that aren't our own.

Shortly after ten, we heard footfalls. I placed my hand on Ethan's shoulder. He carefully folded his book and sat waiting. In a clearing no farther than twenty yards away, a fox appeared. It is so often like this in the woods. You are still and expectant for so long, surrounded by ambient sounds that may suggest the possibility of game but almost always end up being the scratching of squirrels or the slow welter of blown leaves. And then, apparition-like, something lovely simply happens. The fox nosed along the trail, alert but unaware of us. I could feel the gathering energy inside of Ethan, the appreciation he felt for the creature. A sight that was completely outside of his expectations, made live and immediate.

It reminded me of a hunt I'd made when I was close to his age, twenty years earlier. My uncle had taken me to Bankhead National Forest in the foothills of northwestern Alabama. It had been a leafy spring, and we'd chased wild turkey for several days before finally sighting one the last morning of the trip. He was a big tom who answered quickly to every little scrape and click on my uncle's calling box. Somehow, I'd managed to spot him before my uncle had. When I'd whispered that the bird was in view, he hadn't believed me. To show him, I pointed the turkey out. For years afterward, he blamed the loss of the bird on my movement, the animal's natural spookiness assigned to the inexperience of the boy my uncle had brought along. It became a missed opportunity for him, but for me, the turkey was a mystic connection. I wanted the fox to be the same for Ethan.

When we got back to camp, my uncle and Charlie were back from their stands and were drinking their midday beers. After a while, we brought out all the rifles and pistols and spread them on a table that signified the firing line. I laid out the Browning .22 lever action. I planned to give Ethan the rifle, and I believed this would be the proving ground he needed in order to understand what the gift meant. It had been mine since I was a teenager, and I thought it was time he had part of that history for himself.

Yet when the time came and the empty beer bottles were placed against the backstop, anxiety crept in. I was not ready to see him taking the rifle in his hands, handling it with the maturity and respect I knew I could trust him to have. He laid his cheek to the stock and sighted, but the rifle seemed an awkward match for his frame. He jerked the trigger and the round winged off into the dirt. I told him to try again, with the same result: a jet of dust where the round had hit short.

I stepped aside, forsaking my position over his shoulder, the place where I was supposed to stand and advise him to hold low, release his breath, and squeeze the trigger until the report surprised him. I became suddenly aware of the emptiness in the litany of marksmanship. I knew that no matter how many times I repeated the particular phrases of shooting technique to my son, they could never mean the same thing to him as they did to me, and that in fact there was a fallacy there that I'd failed to acknowledge. I realized, too, that I didn't want him to have that knowledge. My love of the gun wasn't something I wanted him to inherit. Such a love brought burdens that I couldn't wish on him.

That was the last time I took Ethan shooting.

IT CAN become so easy to construct an opinion about something when the pieces aren't coming together like they should. But congruence is not so simple. There are hidden flaws, always. Those broken lines are where we can sneak up on truth, ambush all the easy deceptions.

This is the memory that interfered with shooting that day with my son: I had just turned eighteen and had some money in my pocket. Now that I was legal, I needed to exercise that legality in any way I could. Surplus military weapons had flooded the American market in the wake of the civil wars in what had been Yugoslavia; they were available in most department stores with a sporting goods section. I drove out to the local Roses and looked over what they had in stock. I had a couple of guns my uncle had given me over the years, but they had lost their luster. I needed something new, something militant. These were weapons that had seen the practiced hands of soldiers. They had real bite. I handled one of the Mausers, weighed its substantial heft. Perhaps it had been blooded. Perhaps it had killed more than targets and mere game. I paid in cash and carried it home.

I had nothing to hunt. I had moved to a small college town where I knew no one. I attended classes at the community college and stayed indoors, watched television, read. I had time to think and get bored. I cleaned the rifle, ran through the rituals of handling it for the sake of possession.

It is so dangerous to become shaped by our family history. The attraction of repeating old sins should never be discounted. There's a powerful physics there that's hard to take seriously because it seems limited by its source in something as transient as imagination. But it's there, real and immediate as the air we breathe. When I first learned of my father's suicide, I wondered what it would be like to step inside a room and know you would never leave it. People often revile suicides as cowards and egomaniacs, but I've never felt that was true. Such explanations seem facile and self-interested. Like Hamlet, I admire the will of the suicide, the furious sense of purpose and the commitment to a private act. A person's death is poignantly their own. It isn't an object lesson.

As a teenager, I thought I was a depressed person, one who lived with a destructive symbiont. I thought it was inevitable that I would face a rifle bore. The actual idea of firing a gun into my skull seemed so abstract that it wasn't frightening. Instead, I saw the trigger as the purest relationship between action and effect. God and ghost.

But over the years, the answer of the gun became closer, more focused and more disturbing. I realized that I had come closer to suicide through the simple act of concentration. I wanted to join the fatal moment, and in wanting it, I had built a different impulse into my psychic makeup. The gun was more than an object. It had become a totem, a door into myself and my father. Opening that door was just a matter of a few acts, so final and simple in their arrangement as to seem sacred.

I opened the action of the Mauser and inserted a single cartridge in the chamber, rode the bolt forward until the brass disappeared within its mechanics. The thing was loaded, absolute. I flipped the safety free and put the barrel in my mouth, leaned my head against the Sheetrock. This was the true and awful eroticism of the weapon. The idea of the gun had bent me to it, hobbled me to a single moment. There had never been another way. The squeeze of the trigger was irrelevant. I was nothing in its magnitude.

THERE IS a basic lie burrowed within all the codified and reasonable principles of handling a gun. It is that the tool handler controls the tool. But that isn't the case. We cannot move through our lives without suffering the many small damages of what we can't control. We are constructed by a chaotic string of events, deep randomness. We are battered by the things we make, and our logic is dependent on frames of reference that are in perpetual drift. The appealing fiction of the clean, professional shot is that it essentially tells a story. The repetition and patterning of those grouped rounds argue for the roles of habit and stability, which of course have very little to do with the way we live.

That day with Ethan, as we drove home, I knew I was lucky that my son was who he was, and that I had the sense not to try and change that. To force the gun on him would have been a double crime, of both imposition and carelessness. Fathers are heartless in what they can inflict out of a desire to be the kind of man they believe their sons will admire. I have tried, instead, to become the kind of man I should be. I hope that he can see that.

I still try to take Ethan to the woods when I can, though we don't hunt or shoot targets together. I think he humors my love of the outdoors, the fly-fishing, canoeing, and bird-watching that are my passions. His love of the natural world is different. He is a friend to any household or stockyard animal. It wouldn't surprise me if he ends up an ethical vegetarian when he's grown. We both wept openly when we had to have our dog Tessa put down. It's one of the few times we've hugged that I can remember.

I talk to him sometimes about hunting, but I never seem to get around to actually planning a trip because I think the idea is more appealing than the act. It's impossible to know what it would be like for him now that he's almost sixteen, how he would meet the challenge of lifting a rifle at a living thing. I'm not sure how I would fare now, either. It would be different from when I was a boy and killed deer. It would be harder. I think that's a good thing.

But I am certain that if he did touch the trigger and ended a life, he would cry. He would weep as much as he did the day our old sweet Tessa died on the veterinarian's table. I'm proud to know this about him. I believe it speaks well of a man to cry for an animal he has killed.

Coaster King

—

MY GRANDFATHER, when I knew him, was two men. There was the one who was my regular keeper, who took me to fishponds and deer woods, who told folktales in the afternoons before we watched *Sanford and Son* reruns. He devised entertainments and backyard inventions that kept me busy after school. We did small handiwork together. We rummaged and collected cans for quarters at the recycling plant. We secretly hacked bamboo from a neighbor's lot for some obscure purpose, though I suspect the truth was that we did it for simple fun. The old man treated me like a son born late in life but not too late to make a difference in who I would become.

But there was another version of him that appeared when he had been drinking. I could smell it first. A burn, an agitation, in the air. Then there would be the glare that held no recognition or warmth. When that was the case, I knew I needed to get out of the way and let my grandmother handle it, as she had to handle so much else. This is how southern families often meet these things—they simply recede from sight.

With such a pairing of personalities, it was hard to guess what you might get from one day to the next. Still, you had every right to expect something incredible and excessive. The day he disclosed his plans for the roller coaster was the true revelation of his madness.

It was hard to understand at first, but he sketched everything in elaborate detail. The coaster would operate along the simple principle of gravity. An enclosed platform that reached fifteen feet in the air connected to wooden rails that angled steeply from the start before a hard, bucking left turn into the long straightaway. The cars would be orange crates fitted with an upright stud used to "steer" into that precipitous left turn. All that needed to be solved was the problem of friction. That's where Taco Bell entered the picture.

"You're going to use old cooking oil?" my grandmother asked.

"That's right."

"Nasty, used cooking oil?"

"I don't imagine they'll be sorry to see it go."

Confronted with such logic, she had little else she could say. Casting a sympathetic look in my direction, she left the room.

As much as I loved my grandmother, I couldn't believe how poor her attitude was. As a seven-year-old, the prospect of building a backyard roller coaster was as wise a course of action as I could imagine. The arc from conception to completion didn't bother me. All I had to do was carry what materials and tools my grandfather told me to. In time, the coaster would simply *occur*.

HE WAS born to a respectable Alabama family the year World War I ignited Europe. The eldest boy of six children (three boys and three girls), he was forever known to his siblings as "Brother." Even as a child he was fond of tinkering. One of his inventions included a baroque-looking chair wired with electricity. When another kid would hop up, he'd throw a switch and the victim would get a smart jolt. They would cry and scream and run off then come back a few minutes later to do it all again. This was apparently prime entertainment in that neck of the woods.

At fourteen, his mother suddenly died and a few months later his father, Bill Sr., remarried a woman who happened to be a not-so-distant cousin. Suddenly, my grandfather was old enough to get work. He was old enough to get out of the house. He hastened to do both.

The chronology is a bit confused here. At some point he got a degree from Auburn University in engineering, but work in that field must have been nearly impossible to find in Depression-era Alabama. So, he decided to get across the country to California the only way he had at his disposal—hopping freight trains. Once he reached the sunny coast he found work as a butcher, a skill he'd picked up working on the family's small farm.

Despite a modest stature, he was an unusually handsome young man. He bore a resemblance to the film actor Glenn Ford and carried himself with the swagger of a southern bon vivant abroad. Women, if the surviving stories are to be believed, responded accordingly. While in California, he developed an enthusiasm for tennis. I can see the trim figure he must have cut: lean, plucky, and agile in his athletic whites. Both jaunty and masculine, he surely caught more than the casual feminine glance.

After a couple of years in the West, he came back across the country, eventually finding work in Atlanta. It was a step up from rural Alabama and still within reasonable driving distance of Florida, where his eldest sister, Billie, had married and settled. She was the closest of his siblings, the two born little more than a year apart. Still, Florida was many hours away by automobile. He found himself alone in the lonely city. It was here, through casual friends, that he was introduced to my grandmother.

The details of their courtship are hard to come by, but one thing is certain: the attachment wasn't mutual. After a while, my grandfather broke things off and took to the road to see Billie and her husband, Stanley, who had just bought a small block house in Key West. It wouldn't be the last time he headed for the peninsula when domestic life started crowding in on him, feeling that Rabbit Angstrom impulse to run decades before John Updike set it down on paper. He got in his car and left Atlanta early in the morning, drove down through the endless summer slough of south Georgia and crossed over the Florida line. He probably sacked out somewhere on the side of the road rather than hunting up a hotel. He grew up sleeping on the ground in turkey hunts back in the northwest Alabama woods, so his young back would still have been able. Eventually he came down into the Keys. The highway had been finished earlier in that spring of '38 after being built over the bones of the old railway line that had been devastated by the 1935 Labor Day Hurricane. It was bright and new and surrounded by a humming blue world.

This was Key West in its heyday. Hemingway, rising to the apex of his fame, still roamed Duval Street, serving as a one-man tourist attraction, though within a couple of years he would leave for Cuba, shedding a second marriage in his wake. While my grandfather wasn't an artist or writer, he couldn't have been immune to the glitz the island offered. With his sister as a guide, he got to walk the sidewalks trafficked with pleasure seekers and feral roosters, an apt pairing, he was to soon learn. The ocean was an incredible turquoise that stung his eyes if he looked at it too long.

The beer and cigarettes were plentiful, as were the women. He even hit it off with Stanley, who with his plump face, carefully combed hair, and trimmed beard bore a remarkable likeness to "Papa" Hemingway himself. When the night at the bars had run long and the evening shadows lengthened, Stanley was often sheepishly approached by some literary fan amazed at the dumb luck of running into the man himself. And would it be too much trouble if you were to sign something, a keepsake to take home? Stanley would sternly take the cocktail napkin to hand, scrawl out the counterfeit autograph and thank them for reading, and if they wanted to buy him a beer before they went along, why that was perfectly fine too.

Aside from their shared love of free drinks, Stanley and my grandfather both enjoyed fishing, though Stanley clearly had the upper hand when it came to chasing marlin in the Gulf. But as with everything else, my grandfather was a quick study, and soon he was a regular on the boat, going to it with the passion that was his default. He came to love the freedom of being on the water, just days in the sun with his future stretched out there along with the soft horizon line.

These days were doomed to a sharp end when a telegraph from Atlanta appeared. My grandmother was pregnant, and he needed to make a decision about his complicity. I'm unsure how long he sat on that question before he told his sister and brother-in-law goodbye before the long drive north, but I can see the difference in old photographs after he married my grandmother. The self-assured smirk has hardened into a neutral expression that turns the camera lens back on itself. It's tempting to characterize this look as one of resolve, though it seems less self-conscious than that, more attenuated, less governed.

The promised child, however, never arrived. There are competing versions of what happened. My mother, who always favored my grandfather's part in a dispute and had a consistently fraught view of my grandmother, insisted that the telegraph was a trap set around a phantom pregnancy. I've always thought this version of events was simplistic and more suggestive of melodrama than I knew to be true of my grandmother's character. I also know that it can be impossible to penetrate the depths of someone else's marriage, especially one that has undergone loss but found a way to endure, even if that endurance is imperfect.

After I was born, my grandmother remained sober, but when she was a young mother she was as dependent on alcohol as her husband later became. There were terrible scenes. I can't know what drove her to this, but I suspect it was far more complicated than a marriage won by deceit. Just as I can't know what compelled her to achieve sobriety on her own, even as her husband slipped deeper into the pit of addiction. People are capable of remarkable heroism, even if their battles are waged in secret and their victories are won by overcoming the most occluded despairs.

It was nearly three years later, just a few months short of Pearl Harbor, when their first child, my uncle Buddy, was born. By then my grandfather had gotten a good job working with his engineering degree as a civilian contractor for the army. Eventually, the military would decide they needed him at Fort McPherson in East Point, a suburb touching the city limits of south Atlanta. This was where he would work until his retirement in the 1970s.

But he was handed more than a job when he settled in East Point. My grandmother's family, perhaps deciding that the coming of the firstborn was proof of nuptial commitment, gifted the couple a five-acre lot off Washington Road. It was a rolling, beautifully wooded tract with big pecans and chinese chestnuts, a remarkable stretch of woods, especially considering that it remained unspoiled within the city district. Over a single summer he built a small cabin and moved in his wife and son. As 1944 drew to a close, my grandmother once more became pregnant, and my grandfather realized it was time to build a more permanent home.

Not long after VJ day, together they laid the last brick in the rambling three-bedroom ranch. It was, in truth, an approximation of the ranch style, belonging more to the builder's whims than any principled architectural design. And the "they" now counted four, though my six-month-old mother likely sat on a nearby blanket and bemusedly witnessed the others' excitement. What they had was impressive, if eccentric. A large front porch that led into an expansive living room with hardwood flooring. Beyond that a long hall that led into each of the bedrooms, with a kitchen at the far end. Then, almost as an afterthought, a den with a soaring vaulted ceiling built catty-corner to the kitchen, almost waisted looking, if you were to spy the roofline from above. There was a huge fireplace in the den too—a huge poorly drafting fireplace that rolled as much smoke into the room as it did up the chimney—but still something you could get warm next to on a winter's eve.

This was where they would raise their family, they decided, which they did for the rest of their lives in their own unsure and conflicted way.

PARENTING PROVED to be unnatural for each of them. Buddy, when he was an only child, had been easy, but when my mother came along, he withdrew and became sullen. By the time he was a teenager, he had become a behavior problem and had to be sent to military school. My mother, anxious for attention, always felt overlooked by my grandmother. Cross-gender conflict would become the standard between my grandparents and their children. My grandfather and mother versus my grandmother and uncle. Two alliances locked in continual domestic battle. As the years collected, the divisions and disputes deepened. Buddy dropped out of college and enlisted in the Marine Corps. My mother drifted until she ended up married to a man largely indifferent to her. My grandparents witnessed their children's failures helplessly.

When my uncle returned from Vietnam, he drank himself to nightly drunkenness, often in his parents' house. My grandmother pitied him. My grandfather, though, was embarrassed. My uncle bristled under the implicit judgment, and just as he had as an adolescent, he began to act out. This time the bad behavior involved midnight ravings, the occasional brandished firearm. Once, a window had been shot out as he came out of a nightmare about being back in combat. Things became intolerable when one evening he grabbed my grandfather by the shirt and slammed him against a wall. After that, Buddy was told to pack and leave, not to come back until he got his life straight, something he would struggle unsuccessfully to do for as long as I knew him.

MY GRANDFATHER was sixty-two when I was born. By the time I have a direct memory of him, he had retired and spent his time puttering around the house looking after his chickens, his goats, and the occasional foundling possum or racoon. Any kind of work outdoors was a reprieve. Though

I was with my grandparents a lot as a child, it's hard to remember them in the same room together. Each had their segments of the house, their shifts. During the days, I became my grandfather's shadow, while from suppertime on I was attached to my grandmother. The arrangement worked well for a time, and I think it may have settled their minds to see that they could share love for someone and not have it splinter and turn against them.

During the summer, my grandfather retired to the yard, where he kept an open-ended canvas tarp pitched and staked like a tent. A big rattling box fan running to the house with an industrial extension cord huffed a cooling breeze. Sometimes I'd sit across from him on the edge of a creaky army surplus cot, chewing on the meat of yard-picked pecans, and we'd play cards or listen to the song-birds. It was only after I left to spend time with my grandmother inside that he would drink and become a different man. I remember his screaming more than the sight of these episodes, a recollection that is recreated whenever I hear the line in "A Boy Named Sue" where Johnny Cash roars, "And now you're gonna die!"

Once he got started like that, there was nothing to do but go outside while he and she, adept from many years of practice, commenced to gut each other. The whole house thumped from the sound of their fighting. I never saw or heard blows exchanged, but my God, the things they could do with their voices alone was something that terrified me. After it was over, a sick spirit of quietness would attach itself to the house, and it became a place completely without light, as if the bricks and blocks and shingles externalized the pain of the people inside. What remained was a silence without peace.

But by the next day, there would be no vestiges. Both

my grandmother and grandfather were expert at recovering from their wounds. All the years of battering each other had taught them how to press forward, to ignore. Breakfast had to be cooked, the laying hens' eggs needed to be gathered. So, we all did our part, made the household run. If I were in school, my grandmother would pick me up and we would have an afternoon snack before I went out to work with my grandfather. Everyone pretended things were normal, which, in a way, they were.

THE COASTER began to take shape. Stilts were sunk and the starting house built. Even before we were very far along, the structure began to attract attention. Kids in the neighborhood, some casual friends, others strangers, started turning up, asking questions and shaking their heads disbelievingly when they heard what we claimed to be doing.

"A roller coaster? Made out of wood?"

"Like the ones at Six Flags? What you gonna call it, Two Flags?"

The questions weren't mean. Instead, they were guardedly hopeful. They'd seen him create other amusements in the big side yard—the six-hole minigolf course and the revolving swing set—and knew they were allowed to play as long as they were careful. The prospect of a roller coaster, though, must have seemed too remarkable to fathom without some irony. Still, for the ones who stuck around for a period of time, they were happy to pitch in and carry tools, scrap, and nails. Like me, they were partial to their own credulity.

While we worked, there was one, consistent question: "Will it really feel like a roller coaster?"

He told us that it absolutely would. It would put fire in our hair and blood in our balls. It would rip through the afternoon sun like it meant to do insult to the laws of gravity and time, and we'd be screaming all the way until the end.

We decided that sounded pretty good.

ONE NIGHT after my grandfather had gone to his bedroom and I'd joined my grandmother in the den to watch TV shows, the project turned abruptly aside. We heard the splintering crash of glassware in the adjacent kitchen; a second later a cry that could be picked out as human only because of its pitiable final note—choked and cut short with a suppressed sob. A moment later the door swung open and banged on its hinges. My grandfather, or more correctly, the man who had body snatched my grandfather, tumbled forward and advanced on his hands and knees. There was no time for me to clear the room before the fight got started. And when they went to it, neither of them left anything unsaid. After a minute, my grandfather grabbed hold of the arm of a chair and dragged himself to his feet. The effort seemed to draw off his desire for anything other than catching his breath. We all stood there a moment in silence.

"Well," he said and crossed the room for the front entryway. He went out and closed the door carefully behind him. Within a minute he started his jeep, backed it up to his camper, and secured the hitch. Without any more explanation than that, he drove away into the night.

A WEEK later my grandmother found out where he'd gone. He had driven all night, stopping only for gas, to his sister's place in Florida. Billie and Stanley had moved years ago from the storied glitz of Key West and settled in a small town called Hernando, a little over an hour northwest of

Orlando. They'd swapped seaside for swampland, but they had plenty of room for themselves and my grandfather's youngest sister, Jeanne, who had her own trailer directly next door. I guess my grandfather figured it was not much to add his own small camper to the family compound, all of them there together these many decades later. Regardless of how welcomed he may have been on his arrival, that's where he'd landed. He spent his mornings by the water, fishing from the boat house, wary of the rattlesnakes and alligators that routinely crowded that part of the property. In the afternoons he'd come and sit with Stanley, catch part of a Braves game before retiring to his camper for the rest of the evening. By the end of the week he'd found an RV campsite next to a large pond with a sandy beach. He drove everything over there and paid his fees through the end of the month, inclined to serve out the rest of his retirement there, content with his beaded glasses of Jack and Coke. That, along with his solitude, was apparently as pleasing a prospect as he could conjure.

When my grandmother got wind of his retreat, she developed a plan. School was out and she was already tasked with looking after me while my mother worked. I certainly preferred being with her than the slow purgatory of vacation Bible school. So I was a firm ally when she proposed to my mother that I accompany her to see my grandfather and convince him to come home. Later, of course, I realized I was an essential element of the adventure. If my grandmother meant to bring him back, she needed the best bait she could find.

It was my first Greyhound bus ride, and it was an endless night tour through the most obscure byways of the American Deep South. I had no idea hours could drag on like that, one green, stuttering, pallid station stop after another, as we lumbered southward. Finally, we had a half-hour layover around Valdosta. It must have been sometime close to two in the morning. My grandmother said she needed to step around to the pay phone to place a call and told me to watch our luggage. I said I would and promptly dozed off.

When I next woke, I was jostling beside my grandmother as the bus began to grind to a stop. Early daylight grayed the windows. Beside the small station I saw a palm tree and beneath it, my grandfather's battered jeep. He stepped down to the adjacent sidewalk to meet us. He patted me on the back and a few simple words passed between them. He wanted to know if we were ready for breakfast and then he drove us to the nearest Waffle House, where we sat down and ate, pretending this was the most expected way to get together after all, a state away and talking about how runny the eggs were.

Because the bus tickets were one way, it was clear my grandmother left Atlanta knowing she would bring her husband home. Once she got to Florida, she made no motion to hold her cards close; when you hold the trump, there's no need. She knew he'd come back for me, and she was willing to put herself through the tiresome exercise if it meant setting things aright. I'm sure that's how she saw it at the time, as a restoration. There was so much pragmatism in the way she went about the effort that you would think she was emotionally uninvolved in the particulars. It was only a few years later, after he died, that those many difficult years broke free inside her, and she openly grieved for what had been squandered or left unremembered.

Afterward, he drove us to where he'd parked the camper and we stood around looking at the breeze riffling the water. I waded out in the sandy flats. The water was so warm that it closed pleasingly around my calves like a bath. My grandparents talked quietly behind me, making concessions, finding a way back. By the end of the week the issue was settled, the camper hitched to the jeep, and we were headed back through the stubborn Georgia pines. I stretched out in the back and slept.

WE FINISHED the track about a week before school started. My grandfather worked twelve hours a day through the deep end of the summer. The neighborhood kids had started turning up again. Now that they could see that the coaster was real and immediate, they pitched in with the natural goodwill and chaos of children given an important task. Their directionless enthusiasm likely slowed the completion of the project, but my grandfather didn't seem to mind. If he understood anything, it was the untethered hopes of boyhood.

I helped lay the final crosspiece and braced the board as my grandfather hammered it in. He'd painted the big nail yellow, like the golden spike in the end of a railroad, he explained to me. The fruit carts were set at the starting house. We climbed up and he took the front seat; I dropped in behind him. His back blocked the way ahead like a heavy door.

"You ready?" he said, turning his head over his shoulder.

As soon as I told him I was, he yanked the chock block aside and we surged forward. I couldn't see the neighborhood kids, but I could hear them whoop and holler. Then it was just blur and motion.

"Get ready!"

The deep left curve was coming.

"Now!"

We slung our weight and the carts gripped the track,

the velocity just taking off in the straightaway. Fire came into my hair and blood into my balls. We ripped through the afternoon sun like we meant to do insult to the laws of gravity and time, and we screamed all the way. Bars of light and breeze stuttered over us as we sped beneath tree limbs before we crossed the long shaded ditch and finally came to a gentle rest in the woods.

He checked his watch.

"Twelve seconds," he said. "Went quick, didn't it?"

"Yeah," I said.

The Cabin

—

MY FIRST trip to the cabin was shortly after my grand-father died. Four hours in the car, coming from Atlanta to Birmingham and then up into the unfamiliar country, was enough time to seed my imagination with mythic expectations. My uncle Buddy drove recklessly and my mother sat fuming in the passenger's seat. Throughout the trip, they bickered without pause. It was usually about his erratic and aggressive driving, though it could have as easily been about anything at all. They always argued with something like ecstasy.

The cabin sits on a tract of private land abutting Bankhead National Forest in Alabama's northwest corner. A converted army barracks, its dimensions are long and narrow, though the addition of a den with a fireplace and a back kitchen adds a domestic asymmetry to the otherwise martial design. A wide deck wraps around the entire north side of the building and terminates on the eastern back end, where steps descend toward a path leading to one of the two small fishing ponds on the property. Inside, in addition to the TVs, couches, and general country kitchen knickknackery, there are eight small bedrooms, complete with brass numbers affixed to each door in case you forget where you find yourself in the pecking order. There are no divided ceilings between these rooms. Consequently, every time you flip over in bed or let go an audible fart, the fact is common knowledge. So, you soon realize it's advantageous not to be audible.

It was dark by the time we turned from the pavement onto the long dirt road, and still there were miles to go. As the headlights shone on departing trails, my uncle would call their names: Double Fork, Turkey Tenderfoot, Devil's Backbone. Each one had a story to go with it. Names I didn't recognize, nor the hunting stories attached to them. Still, it was an immersion that night, as sudden and bracing as any religious waters might be. In a way I couldn't explain, it felt like a homecoming.

"There's a lot of history out there in those woods," my uncle told me.

What he didn't mention at the time was how little use that history had for our branch of the family.

When we got to the cabin, he had to hunt around for where the keys were supposed to be while my mother and I sat in the car. He cussed and slammed the screen door, went around to the back. Five minutes later the interior lights came on.

"Couldn't find the keys. Weren't where Jim Ray said they'd be," he said.

"Then how'd you get in?" my mother wanted to know.

"Had to rip the screen and get at the latch. One of the back windows inside was open."

"Jesus, Buddy."

I left them to argue about the ethics of his means of entry while I gathered my bags and my shotgun and went inside. The space inside was cavernous and dark, so I went around throwing every electric switch I could to get some reasonable sense of the place. There was plenty of family lore in the timbers of the old building, and I wanted the benefit of laying eyes on it for the first time with as much light as I could bring to bear.

THE CABIN was bought and moved up stick by stick to the present property by my great-grandfather, Will Dodd, a man dead long before I was born. I do have some idea of his character based on prejudiced secondhand accounts and a few authenticated facts. He was an absolutist, susceptible to flattery and favoritism. When his first wife died and left him stranded with six children, he married a far younger cousin who was immediately pressed into service as a generally disliked housekeeper-cum-stepmother, though the paterfamilias apparently remained indifferent to his children's satisfaction with this state of affairs. In fact, as my grandfather would soon learn, his previously privileged status as the oldest son held little continuing advantages. At sixteen, wasn't it really better for everyone involved if he didn't strive to make his way in the world alone?

Will Dodd apparently had an addiction to turkey hunting, and the cabin afforded him the chance to indulge whenever it was practical. In those days the place was still largely spartan, rustic, and used exclusively by the men in the family. The exclusivity was part of its appeal. This would have been long before the time when hunting parties would strive to include women in the excursions as a means of bulking up numbers for the sake of supporting hunting as a sport. They wanted to be shed of the "womenfolk," and if there was a little illicit whiskey drinking and poker to be found up there, it certainly wasn't something that needed to be reported to the wives and small children back home. Certainly not if you ever had any intention of being invited back.

Heat would have come from a wood-burning stove, and anything other than rough interior finishing would have been beyond the pale. The hunting party would have slept on surplus military cots and cooked plates of bacon and eggs on the surface of the same stove that provided nominal heat to the drafty enclosure. Years later it would be weatherproof and plush in its cloyingly fulsome way, but in its early days the cabin was intended merely as an improvement on sleeping on the ground. Still, even then, it began to take on a more important role than simply a place to stow your gear while you traipsed through the woods chasing turkey. Men who were invited to spend time at the Dodd place understood it was a local honor. You might go up there to hunt, but you also got to rub elbows with other men who knew how to make the world go around. Lawyers and doctors and sheriffs would come up and put their time in. Sometimes a politician, or at least someone who thought he had a chance to be. Under that rough roof, warming your chapped hands by the stove, dealing out the occasional poker hand, you got to know everyone around there that mattered and how you might make yourself a bit more important by having the advantage of their casual company.

Such an institution wasn't to be passed down lightly. When Will Dodd died he split the inheritance between his three sons: my grandfather; the middle brother, JT; and the youngest, Jim Ray. For a few years the arrangement worked well enough as a kind of time share by default. The cabin had pretty much been an open-ended invitation for the men of the family anyhow, so the transition to the three boys shouldn't have made much difference on paper. Except, that's never the way it is with brothers, at least not among the Dodds.

Jim Ray had gone off to law school and opened his own firm. My grandfather had been bouncing around the country for several years before finally landing in East Point, Georgia, a town that was essentially absorbed by the growing sprawl of the Atlanta metropolitan area. JT, the middle brother, was the only one who'd remained close to the family's Winston County roots. JT was a quiet and simple man content to remain unbothered by much in the way of worldly ambition. He liked to turn a wrench on busted automobiles and sit in the shade of a deep porch in the long, hot afternoons, a mason jar of sweet tea chilling his hand. It didn't take long for Jim Ray to see a man like JT was the way to get what he was after.

Like many men raised in the South of his day, Jim Ray hungered for land. Though the Old South had given way to the post-agricultural New South by that time, these were echoes of more distant trumpets. An aspect of the baronial appeared to take hold of him. He diligently acquired property, but no holding could have the special value of the old family interest. He formulated the idea that he was the only brother in a position to put the kind of money into the cabin that it needed. It was clear that something needed to be done before the aging timbers succumbed. His eldest brother had a serviceable income but a young family on his hands. In the spirit of conserving what their father had handed down, Jim Ray approached my grandfather with a proposal. They would arrive at a value for each brother's share, and Jim Ray would pay out the discrete amounts, so that the controlling interest, and thereby the daily headache of managing repairs and improvements, would be his alone to bear. Practically speaking, of course, this wouldn't affect the established practice of an open family invitation. My grandfather and his son, my uncle Buddy, would be welcome whenever the urge struck them to drive over and chase springtime turkey or hunt deer in the fall. Truthfully speaking, it was really a win-win for everyone involved, as long as my grandfather chose to look at it that way.

My grandfather, however, did not look at it that way. He knew that when money entered the picture, things would change. He believed his birthright wasn't to be traded off for the sake of expediency. In short, he was a man entirely out of his element. When my grandfather refused Jim Ray's offer, the youngest brother resorted to his backup plan. The next time Jim Ray approached my grandfather about full control of the property, it involved a different kind of calculus. Knowing that JT would be cash poor, Jim Ray had bought his third of the holding before he repeated his pitch to my grandfather. This time, though, he had another lever in addition to his majority share. *It might be time to think about some kind of legal involvement, wouldn't it? You know, to make sure all the details were concluded to everyone's satisfaction.* Outflanked by his youngest brother, my grandfather sold his third, rarely deigning to cross the Alabama state line from that moment forward.

My uncle Buddy had no reservations about keeping up ties, however. By the time the deal had been struck, he was an adolescent and he and my grandfather had begun the habitual butting of heads that would be their default relationship for the rest of my grandfather's life. So, there were no concerns of a betrayal of loyalty as far as he was concerned. He'd always looked up to Jim Ray, or "Jimmy," as he sometimes liked to call his uncle. He admired his shrewd business dealings and voiced his desire to emulate his path to success. The cabin became a regular lure for him over the years. And, like a vestigial but necessary part of the plumbing, he was tolerated.

But as soon as Jim Ray had singular control of the place, what was and what wasn't permissible began to change. This is where that mean old dog, Baptist theology, came in and made itself at home. Over the years, Jim Ray had become something of a recidivist where it concerned being "born again." He, like his eldest brother, had hot-blooded appetites for vice, but whereas my grandfather assumed this was simply another part of his slightly rakish personality, Jim Ray had a religious inkling that didn't quite square with his indulgences. Nor did they sit well with his hygienic public persona. As a result, Jim Ray went through a period of several years where he would let a little bit of the old wildness get the best of him, only to have to double down on his spiritual commitment. Finally, he hit upon a means of making the redemption stick. He could change the very thing that led him on to intemperance. The problem, the way he figured it, was the cabin itself.

He decided the old place needed to be born again as well. This meant rounding off all the rough edges, smoothing away what some might call blemishes. It was going to be a family destination from now own. Nothing that was unsafe for general audiences. No drinking, fighting, or cussing. In this regard, it was a true triumph of architecture. By the time Jim Ray got through with what had been the cabin, there wasn't a lick of the old character left. And it had about as much of a resemblance to a hunting camp as it did to a lunar colony. But the makeover didn't stop with the mere carpentry finishing work. Jim Ray unleashed his wife's decorating skills. If there was a thrift store dish set that featured canary-yellow ducks or black-and-white cows gazing up at you through idiot bovine eyes, it was destined to eventually find those cupboards. Big, heavy coffee mugs with "Not Perfect, Just Forgiven" printed on them, that was something

you could find up there too. The walls became a veritable
explosion of twee and pseudoreligious self-affirmation. This
was before the term *prosperity gospel* became the running
joke that it is for anyone with a minimal understanding of
the teachings of Jesus, but that idea had already taken root
as well. Heaving mountains of junk food were kept out on
the counter so that children and adults alike could ransack
the Oreos, gummy bears, and Cheetos any hour of the day
or night. Consumption became its own self-justifying end,
freed of traditionally Christian ethics of material provi-
dence. You were there to eat the bounty that God had given
the Dodds, after all, and it would have been akin to blasphemy to repudiate such a particular benediction.

BUDDY AND I got up well before dawn. I didn't sleep
well the night before a hunt, and the previous evening had
been no exception. My mother still slept up in her room at
the other end of the cabin while Buddy heated some water
for instant coffee and I sipped a can of lukewarm Coke.
He looked hungover, a look I was used to, so there wasn't
much conversation to be had.

Everything about the cabin was still new to me that
morning. I hadn't yet seen what it was like when it was
packed with the whole cavalcade. The Alabama Dodds were
coming in later that afternoon to stay for the long weekend.
That first morning out would be a chance to see the woods
as Buddy wanted me to see them, as he remembered them
from when he had come there as a boy with his father.

We spent the whole day running the ridges, calling for
turkey but hearing or seeing none. Still the wind was brisk
and the tree limbs overhead groaned as they rubbed against
one another. Everything tossed and danced, become a real
pleasure to the eye. Days like that test your defenses against

sentimentalizing the natural world. Even as a boy, I had been taught to be wary of this susceptibility because it could endanger your ability to see things as they actually are. This was Disney's great sin, according to Buddy. He and his hunting friends agreed that the popularized version of animals as animated playthings was at the root of so many people who were adamantly antihunting. While I think this is an oversimplification, I don't think they were entirely wrong. I do believe the deeper damage Hollywood has done to our relationship to the woods and its inhabitants is that people became convinced they can reliably comprehend that separate world and know how to interact with it. Encroachment, even when well-intended, fundamentally changes a place. That doesn't mean conservation efforts aren't important and necessary, but I'm certain that we must weigh our wilderness ethics carefully or risk tainting the essence of what we hold dear. Still, that doesn't mean you can't fall in love with something beyond your reach. Maybe the mystery of that is part of what it means to be alive and to feel—sometimes to feel recklessly.

Coming back to the cabin with a troupe of strange faces soon dispelled any sense of the bucolic. As soon as we walked in, we were assailed by the sound of the TV blaring manic cartoon action. Young cousins dripped from every stick of furniture, hollering that they were bored or wanted more pizza bites. A couple of women I took to be their mothers whirled among them like wrens, chivying the children with tight, cracking voices. We stood there holding our shotguns for a minute; I could see that Buddy was struggling to make sense of what wild amalgam stared back at him. We were rescued by Jim Ray's son, Brandon, who came through the bratty throng and told us to come on and have a seat at the kitchen table. We went on, racked our guns in the cabinet, and followed him back to where we could hear one another talk.

Brandon asked us what kind of luck we'd had in the woods. He sat and listened carefully to what Buddy said about what sign we'd seen. He was probably fifteen years younger than Buddy, just touching the cusp of middle age. Whereas Buddy was prone to impulse and bluster, Brandon was quiet and attentive in a way not typical for a Dodd. As a boy he had been the youngest kid at the cabin and would have looked up to his Atlanta cousin, but it was soon clear that he was his own man and at ease in the family environs. As Jim Ray's only boy, he was the heir apparent, anyhow. His sisters, who were the women I'd seen when we first stepped inside, were there with their husbands, but these men weren't blood kin and wouldn't have any direct claims. They were encouraged to come and enjoy the place, certainly, but they weren't outdoorsmen. And this was still a piece of property meant to be hunted.

Brandon had followed Jim Ray into the law profession and worked in the same Birmingham firm as his father. Studious by nature, he did well in a business that demanded attention to detail and, in this particular case, a deferential manner. Jim Ray, though he had begun the easy slide to retirement, still took an active role in the direction of the practice, and he wasn't the kind of man who had much interest in deviating points of view. Even as he reached forty, it was clear that Brandon held an admiration for his father that verged on awe. Isaac going bashfully along, counting the blessing of being in the company of Abraham, ignorant of their final business at Mount Moriah.

When Jim Ray got in that evening, everything stopped. The TV snapped off as each and all made their way to welcome the patriarch. I hadn't seen him since the day of my grandfather's funeral where he'd stood above the open casket. That day, I knew there was something so familiar about him, though we had never met. Later, when we had gone back to the house to receive all the condoling pies and side dishes, I'd mentioned this to my mother.

"Of course he looks familiar," she told me. "Everyone has always said he was a carbon copy of your grandpa."

The shock of this recognition was genuine. It was true that the physical resemblance was startling, but there was something unsettling as well. Jim Ray was smaller than my grandfather, much like Buddy was, but he also carried himself with a difference. As if he tilted at the world, battering ahead with the force of dogged charm and self-assertion. He was convivial and spoke kindly, but you got the impression that you shouldn't disagree with the man. He was the quintessential southern lawyer. Even when I was a boy, something told me I should be wary.

Still, Jim Ray was as hospitable as I could ever wish. When his immediate family had gotten through with their hugs and backslapping, he came to talk with Buddy, my mother, and me. The cynic in me today may have looked at this special aside as his stab at noblesse oblige, but perhaps that is too sharp. His joy in being expansive was likely sincere. It's easier to be a good winner, after all. Here he was on the family property, unthreatened, free to be as charitable to his less successful relatives as he wished.

It didn't take long for the natural familial accord to feel its strain, however. That evening after supper the clan split along its habitual gender segregation. The women and children went down to the other end of the cabin to sit on the couch and talk while the television played in the background. The men, though, settled into what would be several hours of nickel-and-dime poker. Real gambling wasn't permitted, as that butted up against some bylaw of scripture, I was told. But as long as what crossed the table amounted to no more than loose change, then your salvation remained unthreatened. That didn't dispel any of the competitiveness, however. Any gathering of Dodd men around a gaming table and you could be assured shouts and accusations of cheating directly ensued. Even though I was only watching, it was clear that they all thrived on it. It didn't take long before Buddy began to slip off to the back porch with his cup of Coke to level it up with a liberal splash of bourbon. I saw too the glances exchanged across the table by Jim Ray and Brandon.

The evening unspooled, and with each new refill, so did Buddy. Like many drunks, he held his liquor poorly. He'd been staggering and slurring for the better part of an hour when he got another rotten hand and he slapped the cards down, crying "Goddamn it!" loud enough that you could have heard him from the other end of the cabin. I could feel the air tighten. They finished the hand before calling it a night.

I FOUND out later that Buddy had been taken aside the following afternoon. The rules of the place clearly needed to be explained. It was a family place, after all. And they just didn't agree with drinking. That was absolutely not the kind of thing that they would tolerate. He accepted the correction sheepishly, though he and they must have known there was no way he could stop drinking while he was there, merely become more furtive. He started carrying a flask out in the woods, sat there with me listening for turkey while he quietly drank until he became red-eyed.

By that time in my life, I already knew what it was like to

care for a drunk. My mother regularly freed her weekends by sending me to Buddy's. Later, she would claim that she had no idea how bad things were at his house, but there was no way she could have been that ignorant. Even his hunting buddies and casual friends would report back to her that his house wasn't fit for a boy. I became used to his brand of abnormal, and it had ceased being anything that I would consider unusual. But just because I became used to it, taking care of the filthy house, the starving dog, or his daylong blackouts, it didn't get any easier.

At the cabin, though, he was still behaving reasonably well. Just not well enough for Jim Ray and Brandon. The next evening at cards I could see them watching him whenever he went to the fridge for something to drink or out on the deck to smoke a cigarette.

I felt like they were watching me too.

I DIDN'T see the Dodds again for several years, though I'd make the occasional cabin trip with Buddy. It wasn't until Jim Ray had died and deeded the place to Brandon that I really gave much thought to seeing that side of the family again. I'd passed through a Marine Corps enlistment and a bad marriage, just finished an English degree and had started in on graduate coursework when Buddy suggested we head over for the Fourth of July. He wanted me to bring my son, Ethan, along and show him all the things he'd once been so excited to show me. Enough time had passed that I somehow believed that would be a good idea too.

Not thinking anything of it, I took along my live-in girlfriend, Kathleen. She was used to Buddy by that point anyhow, an accomplishment that was no mean feat. Ethan was happy to have her along too, another outsider to have as an ally. I didn't mention my plans to Brandon, but as soon as we came into the cabin's main room and I saw the look on his face, I very nearly got back in the car.

Brandon had gotten older, heavier. If he was one side of middle age before, he'd made several years' worth of strides coming down the opposite side. His Prince Valiant haircut stiffly capped his forehead. His voice was quiet, just as I remembered it, but it no longer had the boyish hush it had when Jim Ray was around. He was the patriarch now, and he was used to the position.

I introduced Kathleen and he said she was welcome, that he'd make sure his wife had a room set up for her.

"That's not necessary, Brandon," I told him. "We're staying down at the little cabin."

I was talking about a rustic place Jim Ray had built on one of the fishing ponds not long before he died. Apparently, he'd gotten fed up with the hyperreality the cabin had become in all those years with all that family. He'd wanted a simple place in the woods again. Maybe he thought he could grab hold of everything the original cabin had been before he'd built over it and made it into a redneck bed and breakfast.

"I'm sure Kathleen would be more comfortable up here with us," he said. "In her own room."

In that moment, all the years of being tacitly treated as poor lost relations came down on me like a hand slapping against a table. I suppose that I was expected to give way then, to shuffle off under the pressure of his infallible moral acumen. Lord knows, he bought into the idea himself. He was the hillbilly kingmaker in that part of the state. Whenever someone wanted to run for one of the local political offices, they'd come up to the cabin, sit there, receive his benediction, listen while he affirmed the inerrant Word of the King James Bible. Just as like men had done with his father and grandfather. Except, I wasn't running for office. I wasn't the kind of Dodd who cared what someone like Brandon believed.

"Come on," I told Buddy and Kathleen. "Let's go down there and get set up. I don't need to be told where I can and where I can't sleep."

I NEVER went back to the cabin. Never desired to. Some years later Buddy suffered a stroke that did such damage that he had to go into a home. I was the only one left that could settle his affairs. My mother had gone under the deep waters of mental illness, and though we still talked some then, she wasn't able to come to terms with what needed to be done. I did what I could to have his social security deposited, his property sold and used to pay out his debts. I called Brandon to ask for legal advice for Buddy's sake. He told me that there wasn't any good solution, and that I'd just have to do the best I could. That was the last time I spoke to him.

I was eventually able to get Buddy into a long-term care place. He wasn't happy about it, and he let me know. He was angry that I'd sold his guns so that we could afford to get them there in the first place. He stopped talking to me after that, which, by that time, was a relief.

I did get one more message from the Alabama Dodds, though it was from Brandon's wife, not Brandon. Buddy had busted out of the home where he'd been, somehow hitch-hiked over to Birmingham because he was sure Brandon could help him somehow, set him up in a spare room or maybe even let him go up to the cabin for a while. It was clearly some quixotic nonsense like that. Buddy always believed in the family connection, despite all he'd done to damage it. He didn't understand Brandon like I did. Because when Brandon refused to see him, Buddy walked out in front of a speeding bus. Sounds like a bad TV movie, but that was the violent end of the man who was essentially my father. Brandon's wife sent me a Facebook message to tell me what happened. It was about a week later. She said he was in a better place now because he had suffered so much and that all the Dodds prayed for him.

I never answered her.

Bethlehem Bottoms

—

WHAT WE made of the deer woods come September amounted to pure religion. Better and deeper than that really, since we were pretty much a godless bunch. Heathens hatched straightaway to bloodier purpose than could agree with the plain ceremony of grape juice and soda crackers at the Baptist church we sporadically attended. Attended not out of social advantage or articles of worthy faith, but so we could use the church's kidney pool a few blocks away, a donated scoop of over-chlorinated grace in the Atlanta summer, gifted to the flock when some good layman had passed along heirless. Understand, we were weak to the malice of July. Our willfully unredeemed state succumbed to the city heat, dragging us to enough Sunday services so that we could sneak onto the member roll and splash through until the end of August.

But that was a necessary sin of summer. When the pool closed, our minds bent toward wilder dreams. It was time to go scouting, to tour the game trails, to see what could be seen of the wooded world and how our prey would move come the opening of gun season.

An hour's ride on I-75 south, and we landed on a green-and-red planet, brakes and clay banks. A muddy ooze of undrained bottomlands picketed by rotten stumps, fronted by the remnants of a sharecropping society still wheezing along in this last decade of the century, corn patches engirding shotgun shacks up on blocks, hounds haunting whatever shade could be haunted. Black hands lifted as we drove past. Dust tore out like long tongues from our hunting van's quick tires.

The property was a lease from an unseen old man named Spruce, and much of it had been bush hogged over a decade or more before, leaving an unwholesome snarl of scrub pine and tanglefoot that thrived with rabbit, quail, and, during the height of the day, bedded white-tailed deer. From the edge of the scrub, bigger timber succeeded, white oaks and poplars, pitching toward the south end of the Bethlehem Bottoms lowlands, where the water stood waist deep and held poisonous cottonmouth snakes and other such generally unsavory tenants. It was pure shotgun country, a puzzle of clenched tree branches and vine that drooped like the lank ends of an old woman's unbound hair.

The way into camp was posted with No Trespassing and hunt club signs, access limited by a taut pair of industrial cables strung between two pine trunks and linked with a heavy-duty Master Lock. It was a symbolic barrier, in truth. Nothing a pair of bolt cutters wouldn't dispose of in a matter of a second or two. But its presence was a confirmation that we entered untrafficked territory, and any bodies we might find poaching our lease lacked the benefit of motorized escape. We were a paranoid group, and often we had right to be.

As a point of fact, our original involvement in the hunt club met with no small degree of controversy. The man who held the lease, Jack Johns, was a close friend of my uncle's. Jack held memberships in more than one hunt club around the central and southern part of the state, so he was often away from the Bethlehem Bottoms tract putting in time at one of his other stands. To limit his overhead expenses, he'd subleased the acreage to a trio of country toughs with the surname of Rainwater. I was never sure the exact measure of their kinship, but they were all tall, broad, and tacit men with blotchy complexions at odds with the faintly Asian cast of their faces, perhaps part of that apocryphal intermingling of Scots Irish and Cherokee forebears.

The Rainwater clan was tolerant of our initial appearance, mainly because they had no real rights to object. Still, their tolerance was reluctant. They would roll up into our predawn camp where we sat by the pulse of our cooking fire, their big red Dodge bringing the hard glare of high beams. When they switched the headlights off, we were blind to the resuming darkness. They would slither out and stand at the periphery, not really saying all that much beyond the cursory good mornings, their Remingtons levered over their loose shoulders, kind of just dithering with menace. We would tell one another what part of the tract we intended to hunt, keeping distance as much as possible.

They were tree-stand hunters, carrying aluminum frames attached to their backs like the exoskeletons of weird beetles. Once they were in the field, they were socked in for the day, sitting through the long mornings, eating their bagged sandwiches at noon, not coming out until dusk, tramping back to the edge of camp where they'd pile all their gear into the truck bed and drive back to their hot suppers and patient wives.

It soon became clear that the Rainwaters disdained what we were: still hunters. We walked the ridges overlooking oak groves, then moved down toward the swamp where we might bottleneck a buck moving to thicker cover at twilight.

We read signs and adjusted our methods, sometimes pausing for half an hour or more at a time, covering ground, cutting branches to build concealing blinds when we discovered some likely avenue of ambush. The one principle that kept the peace was that we tended to work the hardwoods while the Rainwaters' climbing stands were better suited to the straight vertical trunks of mature pines. They seemed content with this convenient segregation, killing their deer on their side of the property while we killed ours. They believed in putting as many hours in the field as they possibly could while we concentrated on the prime hours of morning and afternoon. They thought us lazy. We thought them stupid.

We had labor to occupy our middays, and this was what eventually drove a hot spike into our uneasy truce with the Rainwaters. A little over a hundred yards away from where we'd dug our firepit and cleared briars for the center of our camp lay the derelict remains of a clapboard homeplace, likely deserted sometime during the Great Depression. While the structure was fairly wrecked, much of the wood was seasoned and still quite usable, provided of course it could be retrieved in whole pieces. The problem was in getting to it through a half century plus of vine and bramble growth that had done its best to seal off access. The only solution that we could discover at hand was a good old-fashioned bushwhacking. We went after the barrier with machetes, hacking hour after bloody hour, piling up the brush in tall stacks that we would later burn, listening to the eager crackling as the green wood combusted.

Once the lanes of approach were cleared, we laid on with framing hammers and pinch bars, wedging into where the square-headed hobnails drove through the boards and into the studs. Since I was a boy, this was decided the safest duty for me. Farther back toward the building site, my uncle and his friend Charlie Danzwith cut dead oaks and some live poplars for framing timbers, the Stihl chain saws making busy but quick work of the trees no bigger around than a woman's wrist. When they needed my help in bracing an upright they would call to me and I would leave my salvaging work, making sure to never come back without an armload of ripped and denailed siding.

This building project of course was not without some general noise. The clapping of dropped boards can carry a good distance through the woods, especially if the wind has lain for a spell. To say nothing of the sawing and hammering. This gnawed at the Rainwaters. One night at the campfire, their displeasure became a topic of serious conversation.

"Did you see the look the fat one gave me?" my uncle said, lighting one of his Camels with the flaming end of a twig.

"I did," Charlie answered, reaching into the cooler for another Bud tallboy.

"I'd say he looked a little bit like he thought I owed him money, wouldn't you agree?"

"He didn't look too happy, no."

My uncle turned to me. "You need to start wearing your sidearm, you understand?"

I nodded, not asking why. He was talking about the Smith and Wesson .22 pistol he'd given me the summer before for my twelfth birthday. Essentially, it was a lithe version of the same model handgun Dirty Harry used to blast criminals into oblivion, carrying the same graceful lines but chambered with a much smaller and more child-friendly caliber. It was intended as a snake gun and as a finishing round should I put a buck down that still had some breath in him. The only thing I'd killed with it up unto that point was a small black-and-white kitten that had wandered up to my house back in Atlanta. I had taken it in and let it sleep with me in the bed, but by the next morning it began to seize in its joints and lose muscular coordination, symptoms of anti-freeze poisoning. My neighbor Gene was a navy vet with a flair for absurd World War II anecdotes that always involved him spraying a platoon of Japanese with a tommy gun. He was one of that odd ilk who despised cats with inarticulate but fervid passion, and was always my chief suspect in the poisoning. When by the late afternoon the cat was still lingering, I took it out into the backyard, placed it in a shallow grave that was little more than a scratch in the ground, and shot it three times in the head at such close range the fur flared and scorched from the muzzle blast. Gene, from his backyard porch swing, had looked on, appalled. He later told my mother a boy my age shouldn't be allowed to keep a pistol. It wasn't safe for the neighborhood.

In the following weeks, our hunting shack began to assemble itself into something passable. It certainly *was* rustic. The general design borrowed heavily from the concept of a permanent lean-to, with three windowless walls and an opened fourth side that could be enclosed by dropping a plastic tarpaulin. The high side of the building was about eight feet from the tongue-and-groove floor to the roof peak slanting down toward the opened side, where even as a boy I had to stoop to enter, so that made it probably just a whit over five feet. There was little room inside. Three army cots could be wedged in with little extra room for anything but shotguns and gear. If the weather was particularly cold, one of the cots could be folded up and a large orchard-style kerosene heater could be brought in, a horrifying engine that roared and burned so hot that the iron stack literally turned red.

The timing was ideal. Now that we were done with the cabin, the rut was on, the time when bucks ran reckless with lust, their cagey good sense pitched aside. Sex was on their animal brains, and we meant to make them pay for their appetites. We supplemented our simple patience with grunt calls, antler rattling, estrous scent—all the conniving we could muster to lure the biggest bucks into double-aught range.

We got a late start that Friday, catching outbound commuter traffic so that we were delayed more than an hour in the city perimeter before we found good speed. By the time we cleared all of that useless asphalt, came into the promise of the Bethlehem Bottoms and rolled down the long, rutted drive to the lease, the gloaming was full on and all the definite shapes of trees were stretched like questions drawn out too long.

We had parked and stepped out before we realized anything was wrong. The tin roof was sharply askew, the corner edge wrenched around and spearing at a false angle toward the sky. The facing wall was crunched inward. As we circled, we could see bright red splinters of busted taillight plastic splattered festively on the grass. Inside the collapsed shack we saw the loosened and frayed remnants of a wrecking rope looped around the iron frame of one of the heavy-duty army cots. We deduced that first an attempt had been made to simply rip the cot through the wall, the perpetrator figuring the walls as fragile as matchwood, not knowing the deep strength we'd put into the timbers, the green poplars framing the structure solidly. Then in frustration, when the wall wouldn't yield, they'd thrown the shift lever in reverse and slammed into it, meeting a resistance that had battered the truck's tail end like it had just been whipped.

That night blew cold, and without the benefit of our shelter we made do with a blazing fire that cooked slowly down to a firewalking bed of coals. We made up pallets in the back of the van and brought in a sifted pan of coals for heat, keeping the windows cracked so we wouldn't suffocate from the fumes. Sleep came finally and in fits. The cold ate into our sleeping bags, making it a joy when the alarm sounded and we peeled out of the insufficient covering. In motion and in the woods, our true purpose claimed our thoughts, and we were again after the deer, stalking them, reading their sign and waiting, always fatally waiting.

Shortly before noon we came back into our wounded camp. We stacked the splintered boards and posts for burning and looked at the telltale smattering of taillight. On one fragment we could see the miniature impression of the Dodge symbol, and on that same piece a chrome framework with a splash of red paint.

"That solves that mystery," my uncle said, tossing the incriminating piece into the firepit.

All that afternoon we cleaned debris from what remained of the shack and braced up the walls with some more scavenged beams from the abandoned homeplace so that we could weather the coming evening in better conditions than we had the previous night. It was hard work done under a pressing deadline, but after working through the prime afternoon hunting hours, we had a reasonable place to lay our heads before we made our final morning hunt of the weekend on Sunday.

We left without taking anything out of the field, driving back to Atlanta for another week of school and work, another week subject to the many sad inefficiencies

and surpluses of city dwelling. At night I dreamed of the
Bethlehem Bottoms and our own poor colony there. The
wreckage of the shack became something else in my imagination, taking on animas and stature. A sense of what I
had lost buried itself in the broken timbers, and I felt a pain
outside of reason, nightmare heartaches being so much
more terrible than the mere waking thoughts they lay on us.
The busted shack became many different places and people
in my dreams. It was the loss of my grandfather, and how
he'd shown me how to shingle patch a leaky roof; it was a
woodland in Bankhead National Forest when I'd seen my
first wild turkey and lost him to sight when he'd spotted me
and dropped over toward a clucking hen on the other side of
the ridgeline; it was too many things to recount clearly, each
borrowing true elements from one another, and all I could
think of was that the Rainwaters had ripped them away
from me, gutted my memories with their absurd meanness.

The next Friday we cleared city traffic in good time and
made it into camp about an hour before sundown. The
shack had remained untouched, and we saw no recent sign
of tire tracks. We had brought a canvas tent this time so
that we could demolish the remains of the shack and begin
building something bigger and more permanent. Even Jack
Johns was going to pitch in by bringing some fresh-cut
two by fours and plyboard the following morning. But our
primary goal was still the hunt, so we didn't work that first
night. Instead, we strung the long rope from the canvas tent
peak, making the rope fast at either end to a big pine tree
and staking the sides with stobs cut from green saplings.
We sat and talked, and I heard all the old stories again,
the good hunts and bad weather, kin gone but remembered
through their supporting roles in these tales. Then later,
when the beer had been swapped for liquor drunk from

plastic travelers, the jungle of Vietnam would become a sullen presence around the fire . . . F4 Phantoms, claymore mines, white phosphorus. Later that night, I would dream of my own war, my own purchase to the rites the men sat remembering, wishing as a boy might for the romance of trauma and survival, the slow heartbreak of stricken innocence. I would clutch at all the memories of pain that were never supposed to belong to me, guarding my imaginary loss like a born-again fanatic, hoping to adapt myself to a quietly broken world that I told myself I understood.

We were up early as always, no mechanical alarm necessary, alerted to our purpose by the showering calls of a whippoorwill at the false dawn. We slept in long johns and stepped directly into our clothes, so that there was little other preparation as we had decided the night before to take in granola bars for breakfast. The coals lived under a fragile gray mask of scorch and ash, so we dumped a pan of dirty dishwater on it to be safe. Just as we were loading our shotguns and circling up at the edge of camp, we heard the sound of a big diesel engine, followed by the lurid strike of high beam lights, striping the tree trunks along the road in as the vehicle came on, an incision in the otherwise peaceable dark.

My uncle nodded me toward the tree line and I took a few steps to find concealment, stationing myself where I could overlook the camp. The truck shuddered to a stop and the lights doused, leaving the Rainwaters sitting in the darkened cab of a blue Ford pickup, looking out at my uncle and Charlie. I remained hidden while the men looked at one another in the predawn.

There are moments when serious violence is a simple matter of logical outcome, when it lacks the beautiful choreography so favored by entertainment outlets. The wail of tense orchestral music fails to play in the mind. These moments are impossibly complex. Moral decisions seem quaint. Instead, the measure of one's idea of self becomes frighteningly primal and philosophically unsophisticated. Whether or not it is the right thing to act is often smothered by an underlying impulse to act at any cost, so that even when one behaves well to avoid conflict there is a corrosive sense of shame and moral defeat. Good thinking, in short, is punished by stabbing regret.

Such complications were emptying themselves into me as I watched the Rainwaters, laying my shotgun carefully against a pine trunk and unholstering the Smith. I moved quietly, practicing my woodcraft, steps light and long, breaking no twigs and stubbing no roots. The air was cold and burned in my lungs. A slight spill of my vapor breath threaded the broken symmetry of the oak and persimmon saplings. I wanted to draw this thin signature of me back into me, to make myself as invisible as I could, to remain a human silence at the periphery of what I was witnessing.

They knew that we knew, and we all watched one another across that gulf. They watched, I hid. I raised the pistol and braced against a pine trunk, placing the front sight blade on the silhouette of the driver. I waited for the moment that would make it right. They could not have seen me. When nothing happened, I looked back to where my uncle and Charlie stood. Their arms were relaxed, their shotguns at indolent angles. They would not move aside. Their bodies were a pledge, a history.

The Rainwaters did not step from the truck, but backed straight up the way they had come, driving back out toward the highway that was already beginning to hum across the emptiness of the swamp bottoms, the distant sound of heavy freight. As they backed away, I felt the slow fuse of adrenaline shake through my limbs, the underlying relief that permitted its physical appearance. I looked down at the Smith in my hand. Bands of daylight came in soft hues and I could see where the shape of the woods was resuming what it always had. I went out to see if I belonged to it.

Southern Man

—

MY UNCLE never had a child of his own, though he married two or three times, the exact number depending on when and where you asked him. His first wife had seen to that when she'd demanded he get a vasectomy before she'd formally set up house. I can't imagine the kind of message that would send as far as prenuptials go, but for some reason of his own, Buddy agreed. A couple years later they divorced and he moved back to Atlanta where he began to take an interest in me.

Most of those first years I remember him from days at the bar. Normally, he'd pick me up from my mother's on Saturday morning and we'd drive over to the Elks Lodge where I'd be kept in Shirley temples and Mr. Goodbars while he drank Budweiser with his fellow Elks and shouted at the Georgia football team on TV. I wasn't supposed to sit at the bar, but no one complained because I was a quiet, well-mannered kid. Some of the men, sensing my boredom, gave me quarters when they'd settle their tabs. When I had a good stack, I would turn around and feed them to the Ms. Pac-Man machine.

By the time the afternoon football games were over, he had a rolling beer buzz and felt expansive. Sometimes, he'd take me downstairs to the big nine-foot pool tables and we'd shoot a couple of rounds of eight ball or throw darts, but more often we drove home in his '73 Cadillac Eldorado, a veritable bastion of a vehicle that you did not so much turn as slew around corners, often clipping the curb.

He lived in a south Atlanta three-bedroom house with long halls carpeted with dark shag carpeting so thick and stiff it practically rooted you to the spot. There was a half bathroom on the first floor with a broken toilet and another full bathroom in the bedroom wing of the house up a half level rise of six steps. A big dirty kitchen was stuck around the back side of a dining room, which itself lacked formal table and chairs but did have a home-built bar made from plywood that had been passably stained and finished. Above it hung several mirrors elaborately tooled with the logos of Budweiser, Crown Royal, and Schlitz. This is where he'd top off whatever the evening drink of choice might have been. Often brown liquor with a splash of Coke, but almost always from a whole handle of alcohol, typically plastic.

For those first few years we spent a lot of time watching video store movies. A lot of sci-fi of variant quality. The later the night went, the stranger and less professionally produced the subject matter turned. Nudity and innuendo took over after about ten. Beyond that, the selection veered into horror and the softly pornographic. Sometimes I'd fall asleep and wake well after midnight to see a looming crotch or spike impaled hand. Usually, he'd be passed out by that hour, either collapsed in his chair or seated on the floor in Judo sitting posture, eyes closed but somehow still maintaining erect balance.

He'd involved me in his martial arts background for a while, drove me across town to a Judo club in Buckhead for regular Saturday practice. We'd been invited to leave, however, when he began teaching students techniques on the side without the permission of the instructor. Now, we belonged to a dojo of two, which was found in what had been the main bedroom. There we'd put down gymnastics mats we found one day set out on the side of the curb to be taken away with the weekly trash haul. After a good scrubbing, he'd deemed them acceptable for our use.

Buddy was small but ruthless on the mat. I was tall but still had the stumbling uncertainty of a ten-year-old. This was an advantage we never failed to exploit. We sparred through much of the evening, which meant I spent a lot of time being tossed and bruised. When we moved on to armbars and chokes, he had particular zeal. Once, when we were about through for the evening, he put me in a rear choke, holding the pressure of his wrist against my carotid artery until I lost consciousness. When I asked him if he'd felt me tap out, he said that of course he had, but that I needed to know what it was like to be knocked out so I wouldn't be afraid of it happening in the future.

HE ALWAYS said that it was foolish for me to entertain a career in anything but real estate appraising. This was because he was set up in his own small business after having worked under his best friend and perpetual tormenter, a man named Jack Johns. But now that Buddy had struck out on his own, he hatched imperial designs. I would be heir to his conquest. He even had business cards drawn up advertising Dodd & White real estate appraisers. He considered this a great charity to his sister, my mother, a woman with whom he rarely managed a civil word. Regardless of her attitude on the subject, she continued to send me his way when it was convenient for her.

Summers proved to be one of the most convenient times. It also gave Buddy the chance to deliver some on-the-job training, as well as his version of worldly wisdom. We drove through different subdivisions and he would try to teach me different floor plans. I was a slow learner, however. All I seemed to be able to see were reproductions of midcentury geometries, sometimes level, sometimes stacked, but always behind blank doors and bland windows that seemed as remote as if they had been stuck on the other side of impossible.

Once we came to a designated house, he pulled to the curb, took a quick shot of whiskey from his coffee cup then followed it with a chaser of Scope. Thus braced, we'd go up and see if anyone was going to answer when he rang the doorbell.

A lot of his work involved HUD houses. He was out there to give the official word to the bank that any future financing would be valid. His appraiser's license putatively qualified him to determine the worth of another person's home. Many of the residents were Black, and this immediately made them suspect in his eyes. You could tell that he enjoyed the way his appearance in their neighborhood made them nervous, which was only somewhat allayed once he told the residents his business.

"We won't be but a few minutes," he'd say. "Just got to get a few measurements and some pictures."

Once we were inside, we would work efficiently. I held the end of the measuring tape while he reeled off the dimensions, recording each wall span, door gap, and window emplacement on his clipboard of fine graph paper. Sometimes the occupants would watch, but mostly they went on to some other room of the house, having no desire to see how this stranger estimated the value of the place where they built their marriages, raised their families. He would thank them for their time on his way out the front door to snap the required views of the exterior and the street. By the time we got back to the car he would be shaking his head in some private joke of his own, telling me that it was absolutely shameful that people could live like that. No better than animals, he told me. I said nothing because I had no idea what he was talking about.

ONE WEEKEND he told me he had saved a feral cat from the Elks Lodge. The problem was that once he cornered and caught her, he had made the mistake of letting her loose in his car. She had immediately slipped beneath the dashboard and disappeared there completely beyond reach. He figured he could wait her out. Three days later and she still hadn't turned up. When he drove around, he said he could hear her somewhere up there, and that we just needed to be patient.

After a week, he began to become irritated. He ran his arm up under the dash as far as he could, but all he got for his trouble were a few quick slashes. Finally, after she'd had enough of the fruitless back and forth, he snagged her and took her inside. She was an unusually small black-and-white cat, with markings that are commonly called tuxedo. Her thin yellow eyes blinked at us with bottomless hostility, but when a dish of wet food was set before her, she immediately forgave us. Underneath it all, she was a typical cat.

She remained nameless for several weeks until we noticed something changing in her physically. Her middle was steadily growing. Thereafter she was known as Mama Cat and she immediately had run of the house. Buddy became uxorious, tending and coddling. When the kittens came he called me at my mother's house, held up the receiver so that I could hear the gentle mewing.

For several weeks he remained regular in his attention. But at some point, he simply forgot them. He had let Mama Cat out in the backyard and she hadn't come back. He stopped feeding the kittens, I guess, because when I came over one Friday, I found their bodies curled in different corners of the house, left there for several days. The house reeked of shit, piss, and corruption. I cleaned up as best I could and carried their remains out in a big black garbage sack.

ONE MORNING he picked me up and I could see that he was already in the deep end of a bad drunk. He said he had to snap a few pictures to finish up an appraisal and then he'd take me to lunch. When he pulled up to the curb with a scrape and crunch, I asked him if I could stay in the car. He said that was fine in a hoarse voice, and I realized then that he had been quietly crying. He touched the back of his hand against the sides of his face, hit his whiskey and Scope chaser, then staggered out with his camera. I watched him as he stood there and stared a long time, as though he'd forgotten what had brought him to that place. Eventually, he stuck the camera to his eye and took the house picture. He started to cough with that rolling smoker's cough that he had until he brought up bile. He stood there a moment, pinched his nosed then eased into the driver's seat. We rolled forward.

"Do you know what that bitch did?" he said, crying openly now.

"Who?"

"Jeanette, who else?"

Jeanette was a woman he'd been dating for three or four weeks. She tended bar at one of the places in Decatur where Buddy liked to drink in the afternoons when he had time between appraisals. He'd taken me over to her apartment the weekend before for a barbeque. I played basketball with her two teenage boys and listened to their stories about what drugs they'd tried and how much pussy they'd hit that summer. They'd told me that pussy was pink. Then we'd played some Atari.

He told me while he drove that she had called him the night before to ask for money for an abortion. He, who had long ago been sterilized, was not the father, of course. But she had said that he offered her the only chance she had to come through things, and if he had ever cared about her surely he could see that.

"We just broke up last week," he said. "And now this."

Even as a kid, I considered asking him why he thought it was his problem, but I wisely kept quiet. I was used to seeing Buddy out of control because of drink, but this was altogether different. It felt like I was dealing with a dangerous child. Somehow, he managed to keep the car in the lane until we pulled up to the curb of his bank. He left me in the idling car while he stumbled inside. In a few minutes he came back with a cash plumped envelope and tossed it to me.

"Count it," he said.

My thumbs flicked through the trim stack of twenties.

"Five hundred," I said, placing the money in the center console.

"Okay then."

He turned up the radio. Something southern, slow, and self-pitying against the Atlanta traffic. Maybe a quarter of an hour later we pulled into the parking lot of a bar and lounge that advertised pork sandwiches and hamburgers in the plastic sign out front. It was clearly a place that had seen better times, as had those few day drinkers who were sitting by the dim lights within.

"Here," he said, peeling off a ten-dollar bill. "Go get some quarters out of the machine and play some video games. I'll send one of those big hamburgers over."

I walked down to the gaming alcove and filled my pockets with quarters, began racing a motocross tournament while he sat at the bar and ordered a shot of liquor and a beer chaser. The next few hours proved to be nothing short of Dostoevskyian. Buddy absolutely paraded his sorrow. Whenever someone he knew, well or vaguely, sat down for a drink, he would tell the whole story, tears and all. He would demand of them to tell him what kind of woman did something like that, and when they would merely shrug and try to sidle away, he would declare them a good friend to stand by him in a time like this and buy them a round of whatever they were drinking.

Eventually, I could see twilight pressing in on the tinted windows. The hamburger had never turned up, and I was hungry, though not hungry enough to say anything to Buddy. His drinking buddies had come and gone in shifts, easing off their stools and declining to return when even they couldn't bear the depths he freely indulged. Around the tail end of happy hour, his friend Dwayne came in and saw what state he was in. The bartender had cut him off some time before, but he was still conscious somehow, methodically working through a pack of unfiltered Camels and not touching the cup of stale coffee that had been set before him.

Dwayne came over to check on me.

"Hey," he said. "Your momma know you're down here?"

When I said that she didn't, he told me to go out to his

truck and wait for him while he went and talked with
Buddy. I preferred not to wait around to see what kind of
conversation that might have been.

MY MOTHER and Buddy argued over what had happened.
Of course they did. They never tried to tone down their
mutual hate. I wouldn't know anything about it at the time,
but later my mother would tell me when she was on the
cusp of adolescence Buddy had sexually molested her. It
certainly explained a lot of things I'd felt but never been
able to concretely identify. Despite this, and despite the way
he'd taken me along with him to the bar that day, she continued to send me his way on the weekends.

His house had always been messy, but increasingly it
became unlivable. He had brought more stray cats in, but
he hadn't bothered with litter boxes. Their filth was so overwhelming that his few friends from the Elks Lodge refused
to come in. The police were called for animal neglect, but
nothing more than the occasional citation ever came of it.
His bed, and mine, were soaked with cat urine and grimed
with feces.

Around this time, I became fascinated by his pornogra-
phy. Like everything else in the house, it was a material that
he hoarded. His bedroom along each wall with magazine
stacks three feet high. There were milder iterations—
Playboy and *Penthouse*—but there was plenty of hard stuff
too. Glossy bodies splayed and probed. Anatomies rendered
in violent colors. Pink, welted skin. I paged through
magazine after magazine. I took whichever ones I wanted
and hid them in my backpack to take home. There was no
way he would ever know he was missing one of them.

He occasionally went on a blind date someone would set
up for him. The women were younger and they always had

small children. Often, he brought me along so that I could run interference with the kids. He would drink too much before he met these women, so by the time the evening was coming to a close he would tell them how beautiful they were, how much he was in love, frequently calling them his "little one." They rarely agreed to a second date.

The more Buddy struggled with women, the greater it seemed to affect his appetite. When he was drunk or sober, he ogled any woman he saw on the street. Though he never said anything to these women, he had the kind of look that would make them uncomfortable. Even at middle age, he had fully committed to his career as a dirty old man.

Years later, when he came to visit for a Christmas in western North Carolina shortly after I separated from the Marine Corps, he came back from a beer run around the corner. When he came back with a couple of six packs, he told me to fill up his eggnog and bring it out to the back porch. When I went out there beyond ear shot of family, he smirked as he lit his cigarette, said I wouldn't believe the piece of ass he'd just seen down at the drive-thru beer store.

"Just a little ole college girl," he said. "But assy. When she rang me up, I told her if she wanted to make more money in fifteen minutes than she did in a week, I was willing to make that happen."

ONCE I was grown, Buddy and I were always falling in and out of contact. After my divorce, trying to make time for my son while also a college student, it was easier than ever to let his calls go unanswered. Despite everything, I've never known someone so desperate for other people as Buddy. Hemingway once said of his father that he was a sentimental man, and that like all sentimental men, he was cruel. Buddy too was given to easy tears, especially when drinking. But, beneath the hurt, the blade was ever ready. Whenever you left yourself open to him, there was a damn good chance you were going to pay for it.

The last time I saw him before his stroke which would lead to his confinement in a nursing home, he had come up to a cabin I rented with my live-in girlfriend Kathleen. We were both teaching as low wage visiting instructors at the university. During the fall and winter we heated the place with wood we brought down from the side of the mountain and burned in the wood-burning stove. It took a lot of regular labor, but it made for an affordable utility bill. He said that he wanted to bring up his chain saw so that we could work the hill together and knock out the work in half the time.

We spent the entire Saturday felling and sectioning whatever trees we saw that were standing dead. The incline was steep so when we didn't have to carry the cut timber far, just pitch it down and let gravity accomplish the rest. It was good work, and we both enjoyed the chance to do something like that together. Once we had enough to get through the next several weeks, we went down behind the cabin where we could split and stack the logs. Buddy fetched a couple of tall boys of cold beer and we began to drink as we worked our way through the stack.

By suppertime, Buddy had moved on to a handle of rum he mixed with cans of Coke. I kept after beer while I boiled some red beans and rice and pan browned several links of spicy Italian sausage. Twilight can come on in the swift way it does when you're in the lee of a mountain, so Buddy busied himself building up a fire in the woodstove. In a few minutes it began to pop with heat and the whole cabin became a fragrant and snug place to be on a chilly evening. It made me nostalgic to sit there with him like that, reminded of so many nights we'd spent huddled together in claptrap deer camps. Despite it all, he was such a part of who I was that I couldn't ever entirely repudiate him no matter how much I wanted to. I had always wanted to admire the same things he did, be moved by what he was moved by, though for a long time I knew we could never find a lasting peace with each other. Peace could only come at the price of a lie, and I no longer wanted to live under such a burden.

Kathleen and Ethan came in when the food was ready. I set the plates and served, saw Buddy stumble as he pushed back from the table to get to the refrigerator and recharge his glass. He asked me if I wanted one, but I told him I was fine. I tried to avoid the look Kathleen was giving me because I knew she was right. It wasn't going to get better on its own.

As we sat there together and he drank with that increasing thirst that drunks possess, he began to grow irritable. Later, when Kathleen and Ethan had gone to their bedrooms and I told him that I was ready to go on to bed, he said I should sit there and visit with him for Christ's sake. He'd driven all the way up from Atlanta, after all. When he went out to get another load of wood, Kathleen pulled me aside.

"You know he can't drink anymore, right?"

"Yeah, okay. I'll take care of it. Go to bed."

Before he came back in, I took the rum and stashed it in a towel closet in the bathroom, tried to cover it up. At the last second, I thought to grab his car keys and stick them in there as well. I had just sat back down when he toted in an armload of wood and chucked it into the already roaring fire.

"There," he said. "That should last us a while."

He sat down and began running through one of his hunting stories that I'd heard several dozen times over the years. I didn't tell him I knew exactly what he was about to say. It felt like we were coming to the crux of something, and I wouldn't forfeit the role I'd played in our family theater until I knew it was absolutely necessary. By the time his highball glass was empty, I knew we'd come to it.

"Where's the goddamn liquor?" he said when he saw it wasn't in the freezer.

I knew he'd begin shouting as soon as I told him what I'd done. But even as he did, I heard little more than noise. The years had numbed me to his tantrums. We'd played through similar scenes many times when I was a teenager. Often he was fresh out of the hospital where doctors told him he was playing with his life, swearing to my mother that he would set alcohol aside as long as I could come stay with him for the weekends. Invariably, after going over, I'd find the bottles stashed, usually not very well. One time when I was maybe twelve or thirteen, we had gone deer hunting toward the end of the season. In the middle of the night he dragged me out of my bunkbed, told me to find his goddamn bottle because he knew I'd done something with it. He was right. I'd gone out beyond the camp perimeter and dumped the whiskey down the privy. But while he roared and ranted, I never confessed to have any idea what he was talking about. I stumbled around the edges of camp, shone the flashlight out into the encircling dark until he finally went back to the shack and passed out just as morning twilight appeared.

Standing in my kitchen, I realized that he'd grown furious while I remembered that. He probably thought I had ignored him, and perhaps I had. In those few moments, he'd closed on me, balled up his left fist, and shook it under my chin. There were tears of rage in his eyes. He wanted his keys he said. He wanted to get as far away from me as he could.

It was irresponsible, but I went to the closet and gave him

the keys and the bottle. Told him he could go to hell and drive back to Atlanta. He stood there a moment, looked down at what he'd desired, keys in one hand, bottle in the other. Then he sat at the table and drank directly from the bottle.

"Don't you know that you're the closest thing I'll ever have to a son?" he said. "Don't you know what that means to someone like me?"

I didn't see a reason to answer, but I pulled out another chair at the table and sat. I wanted him to quiet down so that Ethan wouldn't be woken and have to hear something like this. If listening to him was what it took, I was willing to outlast him. What he said was hard to follow, largely because I was past the point of caring, but I remained there, nursed my beer for the better part of an hour. It must have been after two in the morning before he began to show signs of nodding off.

"I wanted to ask you something," he said, momentarily clear-eyed. "You're doing all this writing now. That's what you're studying at the university, so I guess you must be pretty good at it. Do you think someday, you might want to write about some of my experiences, you know, as a southern man who went out and did what he did? Went to Vietnam, built a business for himself. Overcoming everything. I think it'd make a hell of a story."

We were quiet, sitting there in the dark and slumbering house for a long time. The wood-burning stove rumbled with heat within. It was a sound like what a peaceable heart might make if it were something that could live on its own in a physical world far kinder than this one.

"I don't know," I told him. "I don't really think that's the kind of thing I know how to write."

Apart

—

SHE HAD me between her first and second divorce from my father. From what I remember being told, it was a short-lived interlude, punctuated by his spending the afternoon and evening of my delivery at an Irish pub around the corner from the hospital. This last detail may well have been a stitch of embroidery on my mother's part because I can't remember seeing any Irish pubs in the vicinity of South Fulton Hospital when I grew up on the south side of Atlanta. But she had a version of him that she brought out whenever I asked the odd question about the man. It always involved his love of drink and all things from the emerald isle. So, whether it's factual or not, her portrayal did seem to cauterize her idea of him in such a way that I've always considered it to be true.

Regardless of her credibility where it concerned my father's character, I do know that the twice visited divorce is true. It was a strange piece of information to carry around as a kid. Stranger even than my father's absence when confronted by the everyday reality of my friends' fathers, who were actual and slightly intimidating realities. It seemed like a detail best kept to myself. There was something shameful about the whole thing. Perhaps because I had no other ready name to give it. A lot of those years were informed by this sense that I bore guilt for events I couldn't account for. It made me feel, even as a boy, that my back was hard against a corner.

My mother worked for the labor department downtown when I was small. I remember her leaving early in the morning when it was still dark outside and I would be left with my grandparents. When she would come back to collect me for our drive back home, it would often be dark once more. The hours between seeing her were a whole country unto themselves. My grandparents made a fuss over me, and I thought it was a fine thing to be fussed over. When I went back to our place (and there were several over the years), the rooms would wait silently for us, and the only thing we did to disturb the quiet was turn on the television and let it run until it was time to sleep.

Sometime after I began school, she began to have trouble at work. She complained about her colleagues and the downtown commute. I remember her saying the word "layoff" a lot when I had absolutely no idea what it meant. She complained of headaches and would sometimes stay home for the day. Often, it was easier for my grandmother to take over for several days at a time. I had my own bed in my grandmother's bedroom. It was always infested with cats, which was reason enough for me to prefer it.

She lost her job eventually. Maybe she quit. Still in her early forties, she had begun to have a series of physical complaints and it made it hard to hold a steady working schedule. There was a little money coming in from my father's social security after his death, and I learned years later that my grandmother gave her money to help raise me, amounting to enough to get by, though just barely. After a while, she began working retail in a department store. I still remember the nearly concupiscent thrill of her Friday paydays when we *knew* there was money in the bank. The desire to spend it was a physical urge, and we both delighted in eating out at the local Chinese restaurant. After, she would buy me toys I wanted despite a filled toy box and get something for herself—shoes maybe, or a bottle of perfume. This was years before I'd ever heard anything about scarcity theory and how it wore down a person over time and remade them into a mere economic battery. All I knew at the time was the desolation that set in once the money was gone and we had another long week ahead before a day's feverish spending.

When I turned fourteen, I got a job bagging groceries. My grades in school had already begun to slip toward middling, and the direct exchange of labor for value immediately overtook my attention. After a year, I was struggling in my classes but had advanced to cashier. Around this time, I began to read about homeschooling laws in Georgia, which were largely undemanding. As long as a parent signed off on the option with the state and agreed to maintain an attendance log, I could avoid the truancy office. I commenced a steady campaign to persuade my mother to let me self-direct the last two years of high school. I told her I would take care of everything. I would read her leftover textbooks from when she'd made an unsuccessful stab to finish college. I would make certain I didn't fall behind. All I needed from her was her monthly signature. When she agreed, I was stunned. The next day I asked my supervisor if I could get more hours.

The next couple of years I worked between thirty and forty hours a week. I would have gladly taken more, but the grocery store capped hours so that they weren't obligated to extend permanent employment benefits. Still, it didn't take long to understand how repetitive the work was and how what came home in the paycheck didn't seem to equal the effort I'd put in. When I came home, my mother was often back in her bedroom with the door closed. She was working only part-time then, usually moving between jobs every few months.

Once, in the middle of the night I was awakened by the stirring red light of an ambulance in the driveway. It would be the first of many similar scenes—EMT's briskly moving through the house, the eerie crackle of radio dispatches on their hips sounding a cryptic string of numbers and acronyms. My mother had already been loaded into the back of the emergency vehicle; I could see her on the gurney by its interior light from my bedroom window. I pulled on my shoes to check on her and on the way out found my grandmother standing in the kitchen brewing a pot of coffee. She told me that my mother had called her not long after she phoned 911. Some pain in her stomach that had frightened her. She would be taken to Grady Memorial downtown, but there was nothing for us to do but wait. She told me to sleep if I could. I went to the front window and watched the ambulance leave.

THAT FIRST ambulance had been for a gall bladder on the verge of rupture. Sickness clung to the house while she recovered. She was put on injectable pain medicine but couldn't bring herself to self-administer. She said I needed to give her the shots. The idea of doing so held little appeal. The doctor told me I should practice plunging the needle into the skin of an orange. This advice didn't inspire confidence.

This was the first time that I remember her being prescribed heavy pain medication. Certainly, the surgery warranted it, but while alcohol never truly grabbed hold of my mother in the way it did the rest of my family, medication was another devil that she was soon to know all too well. She recovered and went back to work, but she often stayed home because she was sick and she had to take more medicine. Her supervisor began to complain. I knew about it only because she would talk about how no one believed her, that they thought she was making it up. She asked me if I believed her, at least. I told her that I did.

During what should have been my senior year of high school, she and I made plans to move. She was sick of Atlanta, hedged in by the fact of having spent her entire life there, and I was eager to go somewhere new, to have literary adventures like I'd been reading about in Thomas Wolfe, a writer who wrote about life in a way that made good sense to an earnest and self-important teenager. It didn't seem strange that I should bring my mother along. Rather, I believed it to be necessary.

At eighteen I received an inheritance of thirty thousand dollars from my father's mother, who had left it in a trust when she died several years earlier. This would be the vehicle of our escape. My mother and I quit our jobs and moved to the tourist town of Asheville, North Carolina. It held a place in her imagination because of childhood trips she had taken with my grandparents and uncle on the way to the Great Smoky Mountains National Park. For me, it was a territory as blank as a page.

I took my GED within weeks of getting there with the idea of seeing if I could get a job at Dave Steel Company. I knew it was supposed to be good money for someone just starting out, and it squared well with my scheme to cultivate a rough-hewn Jack Londonesque biography. I had already decided writing was what I wanted to do with my life, and adventure seemed a necessary foundation. Though the job never came through, I did well enough on the GED that the woman who had administered the test excitedly telephoned me and said I should enroll in the local community college.

AFTER A few months of classes, I began to feel the predictable strain to socialize with the friends I'd made. Through them, I met the older woman whom I would marry a few months later. She was twenty-five and I was still eighteen and as unprepared for a relationship as could possibly be imagined. But my self-assurance blinded me to all practicalities. Soon, I was spending most of every week with her, often staying with her overnight. One day I came back to the house I lived in with my mother to find all of my things boxed and haphazardly placed outside the back door. My mother, livid, told me that she wouldn't have me treat *her* home as a flophouse. To get my things and leave.

I drove away, dazed. It seemed that I was witnessing a melodrama happening to someone else. My truck rattled down the road, the boxes sliding in the bed when I took the deep mountain curves. I had no idea what to do, so I drove to the bank. When I got there to make a withdrawal, the teller told me that there wasn't enough to cover my request. I told her that was impossible. True, I'd spent a lot of the money I'd inherited, paying for the move up to Asheville, the deposit for the house, my half of the rent, the year's tuition. But there was still money there; I was sure of it. She called over her manager who looked at the screen over her shoulder. He squinted at the numbers.

"It looks like the other person on the account withdrew thirty-six hundred dollars yesterday afternoon," he told me. "Do you recognize this name?"

Of course I did. My mother and I had opened the account together. I asked for the forty dollars that was still left in the account and drove the only place I knew to go.

IT DIDN'T take long to realize the marriage was ill-advised. Even her mother had advised against it, but I was determined to make things stick. With only a year of college behind me, I needed work that would provide some degree of security. Three weeks after we were married, I rode the bus to Parris Island to become a marine. Six months after that, she was pregnant, and what might have been quickly corrected turned into the long haul.

Ethan had the natural reparative effect on my relationship with my mother. She flew out to California to dote on him, but even a few minutes in the house and she and Ethan's mother were at each other. When her visit was up, I believe that we were all relieved to have the benefit of distance. There were occasional phone calls over the four years of my enlistment but not much else. When it was time to separate from the service, we made plans to stay under my mother's roof while we worked on housing and college admissions. It wasn't hard to see how pleased she was. It was well past time when we should be home, she said.

The past, however, predicted what awaited. The house was too small and we were on top of one another from the minute we arrived. I needed work to carry us through until the beginning of school and took an early morning job loading packages in the backs of UPS trucks. My sleep was hectic and my nerves frayed. When an apartment opened up in the college town an hour away, we packed a truck and were gone by the next day.

Around this time, my mother's health began to suffer again. She developed a palsy that the doctors struggled to identify. She called, often several times each day, to talk about when her next appointment was, how frustrated she was becoming about not finding answers. A hard edge crept into her voice if she sensed that I wasn't listening closely enough, distracted by the needs of the baby or my wife. It was a trait she had always had but had become more frequent since she had told me to leave the house. Increasingly, I had little patience with her stories, and I answered the phone less and less.

My second year at the university I got a full-time job as a newspaper reporter while I continued taking classes. It involved a lot of driving and as much time away from home as I could manage. A few months later, the marriage finally broke apart and I moved into a small furnished apartment with cinderblock walls. I was involved with my own hand-to-mouth needs, and I had to let my mother deal with her own.

As is the case with many others, my estrangement from my mother didn't come from a dramatic break. Certainly, there was a pressure of resentment but that didn't tip things decisively. For me, being apart became a matter of self-preservation. Her phone calls became more continual, and no matter how long I listened and empathized, it never satisfied her. Once, she was involved in a desperate and abusive relationship with a retired Air Force sergeant, and when it resulted in an ugly fracture, she called and tried to explain what had happened, but I couldn't understand her for the weeping. She wanted me to take care of the pain the world inflicted on her. Looking back, I realized it was something I had done for her as a child; as an adult, though, I couldn't. I was no longer able to father her now that I needed to do that as best as I could for my own child.

Of course, looking at the relationship from the outside, my actions could be seen as cruel. I expected and accepted that, even when her friends contacted me to let me know that I was letting my mother down. Though I never said it, I couldn't help but notice they were unable to make themselves directly available as well.

OVER THE years, ambulances came to my mother's home more frequently. The elaborate routine of prescription pills chewed away at her hold on reality. Once, when I was having beers with friends across town, she called to tell me that a man had told her that money was hidden in the walls of her trailer and that she needed me to come over and help her get to it. When I told her she was imagining things, she became irate and said that she would take care of it herself. I heard several violent blows and asked her to stop. A moment later, I could hear her talking to a sheriff's deputy on a welfare check. She hung up.

The next day she called me from the hospital, asking me to visit her and to bring Ethan along. I said that I would and picked him up from his mother's house. When we got to the information desk and I asked where her room was, the woman explained that they had no record under that name. After I laid out the details of what had happened the evening before, she smiled sympathetically and advised I go across the street to the mental health wing, that records of patients there were kept confidential for the sake of discretion.

I was angry that she had called me to bring my son to a mental health unit, but I pressed ahead despite my better judgment. When we were admitted to where she shared a room with another woman under observation, my mother said she was so glad to see us, that we needed to make an effort to come around more often. She talked like someone receiving afternoon company on the front porch. One of the nurses on the duty desk brought in a coloring book for

Ethan. I was angry that people brought children to a place like this so often that they had thought to provide something for the kids to do while the adults tried to talk to each other about what couldn't be talked about. I was angry that she was here. Above all, I was angry that she was my mother.

After the terse visit, I agreed to go to her house and check on her Shih Tzu mix, Gracie. Because I had no key, I slid a credit card through the door seam and worked the fragile lock open. Immediately, the reek of an animal left by itself hit me. A second later, the dog tumbled out of the bedroom and charged toward me, so anxious that every hair on her vibrated ecstatically. After petting her until she calmed, I went to see what the rest of the house looked like. The wall separating the bedroom from the kitchen had a hammer-torn hole as big as a fireplace. The pressboard remnants were scattered along the floor. On the nearby table, something piercingly bright caught my eye. It was a stack of old family photographs, many of them from the late nineteenth century. They were once in an album I had gone through when I was young, learning the faces of the different branches of the family I never knew. I had made up stories about them in my head, so that they had meaning beyond simple bloodlines. But I saw that they were different now. Under the influence of whatever chemical storm had taken hold of my mother, she had cut the photographs from the pages where they had been pasted. She had scissored through their bodies and dashed their features with grotesque strokes of acrylic paint—red, yellow, violet. I swept them into the trash can, scooped up the dog, and left.

AS NEXT of kin, I would hear from the authorities occasionally. Usually, it was to see if I could convince her not to abuse the 911 system. I explained I was as helpless to prevent this as they were. I looked into possible full-term care, but without her consent, it was nearly impossible to move forward. When she threatened suicide over the phone to a hotline, the ambulances were called once more to transport her for observation to the state mental hospital in Morganton. But she was never there for long. Somehow, she always found her way back and there would be silence for a while until the cycle repeated.

Not long after I married April in winter 2012, I got a call from my mother. She said that it was an emergency and that she needed my help right away. We hadn't spoken in over a year. The last communication we'd had was when she told me that my older half sister, my father's first child, had come by her house and asked to see me. At the time I was confused. I'd tried several times through the years to track down my sister but never had any luck. But the idea that she had turned up elated me. I quickly returned my mother's call and asked to speak with her. My mother said that she had left already, that she had been in a hurry. I asked for her number so that I could make contact, but my mother said she hadn't left a number. Immediate dread set in as I realized it was just another of my mother's delusions. I could have snapped the phone in half.

Still, I went to her house to see what the emergency was. As I expected, it was nothing out of the ordinary. Help with her byzantine medications, I think. While I tried to organize them into a coherent order, she began asking about my new marriage, who I thought I was going off and remarrying without telling her first. Who would be so thoughtless? I left quickly and never came back.

WHEN I remember my mother now, the truest thing I can say about her is that she was exhausting. This isn't recriminatory. It merely conveys the effect that being around her had taken over the years. She imposed her need on me from the time I was small until I was on the cusp of middle age. That much time under that kind of pressure didn't fracture me, but it did wear away my capacity to care. Long-term dysfunction is like long-term impoverishment—it grinds and grinds until there's nothing left to give, nothing more remaining that can be taken.

She told me once that when she was pregnant she had hoped for a daughter and had picked out the name Christine. I can't imagine what she might have made of a little girl, given her profoundly troubled relationship with her mother. They would have had their own involuted loyalties and resentments, certainly. I sometimes wonder if my mother held that fictional daughter in her mind once she and I no longer saw each other, pretended that another version of her child was lost somewhere in the world. Perhaps this imagining on my part has more to do with the sister I've never met, the one my mother invoked when she most wanted my attention. Since I've known about her, I've longed for my sister with raging emptiness. Perhaps the shadow she left behind has allowed me to love other women in her place. At the very least, it's not the worst thing to believe.

In August 2020 I received a sympathy card in the mail from a cousin telling me that my mother had died in the long-term facility where she had been living for the past three years. She was seventy-five. It was a Sunday and I had been on an overnight hike on the Appalachian Trail, so I was already footsore and ready to sit quietly for a while, soak in the bath, drink a couple of beers. It was hard to know how I should feel, though I sensed an almost physical blow when I read the news. A heavy thing, I told a friend the next day over a text, even when the relationship was as strained as my mother's and mine was. For the next couple of weeks that gravity pulled at me, made me feel old and careworn. My work irritated me. I drank too much and talked with my wife too little. Sitting down to write was impossible. But then the holidays were on us and the problems of parenting a teenager during the long pandemic year took over. Sometimes, the difficulty of the present is exactly what's needed in order to escape the past, so I was grateful for my current worries and how they gnawed me in a way that I could think of little else.

Months later, a package arrived from the nursing home. It was my mother's last effects. I thought of those haunting lines of Dickinson's: "I willed my keepsakes—signed away what portion of me be assignable." Certainly, this assignment had to be meager. The box was not much larger than what would contain two pairs of shoes. I waited for my wife to come home before I opened it. She likes to kid me that I have so many stories about growing up that she's never heard, so I thought we might find a curiosity or two that would make for one of these previously unearthed anecdotes. We took the package to the bedroom and I cut through the box seam. Inside were several stacks of old photographs. Many faded a sallow tint from age but many old enough to be black and white as well. As we sifted through them, April noticed that several were tacky on the back from the residue of glue or double-sided tape. These were some of the photographs lifted from the big green album I spent so much time with as a boy.

"What's this?" she asked, pointed to a clipping affixed to a photograph of me at three or four wearing an oversized camouflage hat. In a neat cursive was written "Sure do love to hunt with my uncle Buddy." Almost as soon as she handed it to me, she found several others attached to their corresponding pictures. A collage of short narrations, most of them comic, that my mother had written into the album. I had read over them countless times, never marking them as something other than what any reasonable person would do with a photo album. I sat there and read them all again, remembering how much pleasure they'd given me.

I wish my mother could have known that.

Why I Don't Hunt Anymore

—

WHEN I hunted the southern woods as a boy, my first concern had little to do with what I might kill. Instead, I time-traveled. At home during the week, I consumed repeated viewings of *Grizzly Adams, Daniel Boone,* and *Jeremiah Johnson.* But when the weekends came around, a century dropped out from underneath me. My life became the ritual concerns of making camp, reading sign, collecting kindling. The campfire was by far my favorite TV program, and I could stare for hours into its suspense and drama. The most important lesson from the camp was what I could learn from the trails and creek beds and swamp bottoms and how they provided a sufficiency that would be hard to express to anyone who had never experienced it for themselves.

Today though, I feel no desire to pick up a rifle or shotgun and walk the Tennessee ridges and hollows within easy driving distance of my home. It's been close to twenty years since I've sat in a deer blind or called for a tom turkey at daybreak.

This doesn't come from a place of antihunting. I have

believed, and still do, that there should be a psychological price exacted by eating animals. If you're willing to eat meat you should be willing to kill to do so. If we have learned anything in the last three decades about food ethics, it's that most Americans rely on a largely brutal though impressively expedient system to deliver the lion's share of our protein needs. So I maintain a large respect for those who go out to their tree stands to fill their freezers with wild meat. I think they don't let squeamishness cancel out their natural appetites. If more people did so, we would have a healthier ecology and an infinitely more well-adjusted relationship to what we put in our bellies.

I still enjoy my time in the woods. I continue to camp, paddle, hike, and fish throughout the year. And yes, I even cook ribeye steak over the campfire when I go on these trips. I'm even more avid in these pursuits than I was as a boy. My love of nature has deepened, which I think is a common effect of growing older. My desire to experience wilderness on its own terms has entwined with my love for reading about it. Instead of the old Hollywood versions of outdoor adventure that fired my imagination as a boy, I revisit my Thoreau, Emerson, and Abbey, or I dig deeper into my more recent encounters with John McPhee and Sigurd Olson. I've tried to grow in my understanding, become more open to its contemplative parts. Still, this evolution wouldn't be enough to dispel my nostalgic ties to those hunting camps with their many meaningful tales and legends. Too much personal accomplishment is back there behind me to want to give it up.

I have realized then that my change of attitude isn't in the southern woods or my own development but in a large percentage of the southern outdoorsman himself. I use the word "outdoorsman" with intentional precision because the change, though not universal, has been largely male. While there are many who still practice the reverence and respect that were hallmarks of my youthful hunting experience, it seems their numbers thin each season. Instead of the ethic of Leave No Trace, there is another kind of code. On the interstate you see it on the back panels and rear windows of tricked out pickup trucks. Stylized decals with phrases like Bone Collector or pictures of deer skulls against American flags or the graphic logo of the comic book vigilante The Punisher. The pastoral somehow got swapped out with the paramilitary while I wasn't paying attention, and I can't think of anything worse that could have happened to the average hunter.

It's hard to understand anything in the rural South today without viewing it through the lens of reactionary politics and what's supposed to pass for conservative culture. Southern white manhood doesn't know what to do with itself. People outside (and inside) the region consistently ridicule it for its role in racial prejudice, sexist dogma, and overall violent propensities. Some have paid attention to these criticisms, tried to be more thoughtful about how they move through the world while holding on to the traditions that still hold real value to them. But so many others have listened to their baser impulses, lashed out, doubled down.

They've committed themselves to this burlesque of masculinity that has become a new standard of the southern man out in the woods. They've forgotten what it means to experience the beauty of the wilderness. They don't go out there to embrace solitude and time. They go out there to pull a trigger, and they have no qualms about advertising the fact. This desire to show off, to practice vain machismo, it changes everything. The act of hunting becomes mere background to the desire to offend. It is cultural theater, and it measures its effectiveness in terms of its ability to provoke an emotional response, not understanding. It paints blood everywhere it can, often in an Instagram or Twitter feed.

I'm keenly aware of the financial contribution to conservation that comes from hunters' license fees. This is what makes the statistics released by the Department of Interior in 2017 showing a decline in hunting so alarming. I believe a significant factor in this change is that the kind of hunter I write about has largely gone unchecked by the greater hunting community. The problem with rot is that it can be contagious. If left alone, either from avoidance or indifference, infection affects the larger body. The crisis we face as people who care about the outdoors and hunting traditions is a crisis of messaging. It's naive to believe that iconography doesn't matter, even when these images come from the fringes. Fear of scrutiny is cowardice. Ignorance of the power of a symbol is foolish. We have a problem, and it is up to the average, decent hunter to say something about it.

Recently, I canoed for a week with a small group of close friends in the Quetico-Superior region that comprises the border between Canada and Upper Minnesota. Each of us was born and raised in some part of the South, and it was our first time in the fabled Lake Country. We have made many trips together throughout the southern woods, paddling, hiking, drinking, and telling amiable lies. We're all writers and care about the woods. We know one another, what we're about. By the end of the trip, we had noticed something different about the North Country. Not in the woods themselves, which were as stark and striking as we expected them to be, but in the small town of Ely and its immediate surroundings. It's a place that couldn't be denser with sportsmen. Not just canoe paddlers and kayakers, but walleye fishermen and big game hunters too. Most of them big, blue-collar men who weren't shy about a bloody mary and a beer chaser after a full day of fishing on the lake. But there was a pronounced difference between these men and their southern counterparts. When we sat down at the lodge bar with its wood paneling, beer signs, and taxidermized pike, the atmosphere was calm, the company convivial. We got to experience "Minnesota nice" at close range. There was no talk of you not being from around here, no guarded inquiry to the school of politics you followed. These men only wanted to know how the fishing was, how the weather had treated you.

It made me wistful for those old hunting trips. I hope they aren't completely gone, but I fear that brand of out-doorsman is fast going out of style. He doesn't fit in too well with the sloganizing and self-declared Southern Rebels of today with their Heritage Not Hate flags and their Molon Labe stickers. Large groups of young and middle-aged white men convinced they are under assault by a culture shift they want to stop, though it continues to outpace them year after year. I don't believe these men are exclusive to the South, but you see most clearly the things that are a part of the place where you grew up. There's a keenness to where you come from, a piercing sensitivity, and it's hard to look away when you've glimpsed an ugly truth.

In his seminal ecological essay "A Native Hill," Wendell Berry discusses how the way we regard the land affects our patterns of behavior. In one passage, he talks about the psychological difference between taking a trail, which accommodates itself to the landscape, versus following a road, which cuts through the topography with the aim of maximum efficiency. At the extreme edge of this disregard for place, Berry places the highway, a piece of infrastructure designed as an epitome of all things contrary to the natural order of things. "Haste" is the word he uses. It's a good word. I believe haste is at the heart of the problem of the modern southern outdoorsman. Haste to kill. Haste to defy. Haste to prove manhood. He has forgotten or more likely forsaken the patient way of being in the woods. Instead, he collects bones, he accrues points, realizing in real life marksmanship skills he first perfected through years of first-person-shooter video games. He goes to gun shows to buy camouflage face paint and pick up the newest tactical flash-lights while browsing the latest prepper fiction. He imagines himself as a hero, his conceal-and-carry permit proving its ultimate worth when he puts down a mass shooter at his job or campus or church.

Surely, there's another way to be in the woods.

I remember walking with my grandfather in the woods carrying my single-barreled .410. It was a warm autumn af-ternoon, and we were after squirrels. The leaves crinkled like paper underfoot. The sun was clean and strong against the thin sky.

"This way," he told me. "Now it's time to head on to the deep woods."

I followed him, thrilled at whatever mystery such a place might hold.

I'd like to go out like that again sometime. There are many of us, I imagine, that feel the same way.

What We Gain
in the Hurt

—

MY COUNTRY had just taken me back, and I sensed, not for the first time, what it was to feel stranded between extremities. When I came across from Canada, I had a passport in my pocket that showed I'd been away longer than was strictly legal, so I was grateful to be given passage, even if I was bound to suffer the suspicion of the men watching the American side of the border. There seemed to be a lot of bluff going on, something that had gotten more pronounced and paranoid since September 11. Even six years later, they were probably sorting out the best way to perform their genial menace. Stepping across official boundaries has always unnerved me. Even toll booths make me antsy. I'm not sure why this is the case, but the reaction is physically palpable. In that moment, the gulf between here and there seems impossibly distant. But the pressure of coming back into your home country is of another cut altogether. You're going back into all the familiar turbulences you left behind, and while there is a kind of adventure in coming home, there's also this feeling that you've forgotten some of the hard math that reminds you who you are and what you should have become.

I got back to the mountains of Asheville, North Carolina, in the middle of the night after fifteen hours on the road straight from Toronto, and I had little more on me than a single suitcase and an idea for a book. That was part of the risk. The other part was in trying to repair what damage I'd done by going away to chase down a relationship with a girlfriend that had been a long time in its dying. A year in Texas and another in Canada. I had a ten-year-old boy I'd seen fewer than half a dozen times over the past couple of years. Better intentions had been to make the trip back to Carolina once a month, but those plans were eclipsed by several small and predictable failures. Regardless, I was now back for good, and I meant to see what that might mean for everyone and everything involved.

I let myself into my mother's trailer; she had left the door unlocked when I'd called ahead to let her know I was coming in. It was late enough that I knew she'd already be in bed, so I moved quietly to the front bedroom and put my few personal effects away and crawled between the sheets with a bottle of Absolut Citron. I'd developed the nasty habit of drinking through my bouts of self-pity in the past few months, and vodka had become my drink of choice in that period.

The trailer was an excellent setting for depression. The mattress was prickly with feather quills, the walls composed of pressboard. Additionally, I was without a job or a real plan. From where I lay with my simple cocktail, I could see that the neighbor flew a trim Confederate battle flag beneath a sodium light. When I closed my eyes, I could smell the faint whiff of dog shit in the carpet. I drank the bottle down but couldn't sleep.

I ROSE early the next morning and sat over coffee and thawed supermarket biscuits with my mother while she watched television. We hadn't been able to really talk to each other since I'd first started dating my ex-wife, twelve years earlier, and being gone for two years had done no kindness to the break between us. There has always been shame and pettiness in any house we shared and we were at our best when we pretended a different history. She often had told others that she had raised me alone. It was true that my father, when he was still alive, was never around. But I remember being with my grandmother or uncle more than I remember time spent with my mother, though that may be a fault of my partial memory. I can confidently say that she has always struggled to adjust herself to the routine demands of survival. Something in her has never fully developed, caught in a version of the past that only she can recognize, and I have never been able to meet her where she is. I still wonder who has been more injured by this.

She had moved up to the mountains with me the summer I turned eighteen, attaching to my desire to leave home, and somehow managed to come along despite my best countermanding efforts. She had spent all her life in Atlanta, and the mountains and small-town living of Asheville promised something vaguely pastoral and nostalgic. I had begun reading Thomas Wolfe when I was sixteen and was desperate to make a material connection between the hidden power of words and the living, breathing world evoked in Wolfe's fictional version of Asheville in his first novel, *Look Homeward, Angel*. I wanted to be able to write like that, to see like that. I had convinced myself there would be room enough there for both my mother's and my escapes.

In the years since, I've always found myself drawn back to the mountains. I've drifted across the country for much of the past two decades, but it's always been this place, this meeting of sky and ground that writes something permanent in my heart. I wandered the Georgia woods as a boy because there's a sadly beautiful isolation when you give yourself over to the natural world, and that sense is made larger by the age and reach of the southern Appalachian high country. In the mountains, you have the feeling that this is a profoundly old world, rounded off by the soft rays of a distant sun. Menial use seems beneath it somehow. Men have imported all kinds of architectural ugliness to the ridgelines, but that blight is temporary. With all the plaster and presswood they've warped into place, you get the feeling that time and weather will have little trouble dispensing with the thin timbers, the sliding foundations. This belief that the mountains had abided and would still abide was the elastic that kept pulling me back to my adopted home.

And too, there was this idea for the book. After years of trying to find what it was that I should write, I had finally heard the voice of a true character, a man from the mountains, from the hollows and pocket ridges. My imagination had traveled home before I had. Walking the icy sidewalks of Toronto a few months before, sitting over beers in a narrow pub off Bloor Street, I already knew this man who would propel the story, knew his regrets and strength. I started writing and the words were, for the first time it seemed, my own. I had to get back to see what this meant, to see how my story about a father and son a century ago would coincide with the story of what had happened to me as a failed father, and how I might be able to salvage some important part of the future.

THERE WERE no jobs back in Asheville, no offers to teach. I'd run out of a perfectly good PhD program when

I'd gone up to Canada and now I had little to offer other than a few pale efforts at freelance writing, a hope which is tenuous even in the best of markets. But the national economy had just plunged and those lucky enough to have steady work weren't sharing any connections with part-time teaching gigs they might snag for themselves. I couldn't blame them. Most Americans believe college teachers are firmly ensconced in middle-class insularity. They still see cartoons of camel hair and elbow patches, as if the modern professoriate has stepped from the pages of a 1950s *America Scholar* magazine cover. The reality for many college teachers under forty is something radically different. Patchwork employment is available if you drive between two or three colleges, teaching introductory classes on contract, often missing pay periods for long stretches at a time, particularly over the holidays. One doesn't need much of an imagination to understand how quickly this can convert someone into a Marxist and explains why so many teachers are frankly befuddled that much of middle America sees the concept of redistributing the wealth as an inherently nefarious concept.

So I fell back on something I knew well: security. When I'd served in the peacetime Marine Corps several years earlier, I'd been part of a short-term program that cross-trained enlisted personnel in a secondary MOS, an acronym for what is commonly known in the civilian world as a job. While I'd spent most of my time as an M1A1 Tank crewman, I did have the dubious advantage of some law enforcement training as an MP, and I remembered being told that would somehow benefit me down the line.

I had resisted walking a security beat at first, figuring I might find something through a temporary service. The only place that appeared to be hiring at the time was a hard labor company that administered a test before putting you in the availability pool, a test that asked things like if you'd ever been in a fistfight or rough horseplay on the job site and if so, had anyone been sent to the hospital as a result. I decided to answer honestly, which was yes on the first count. It's hard to imagine having gone a week on the tank ramp without some kind of light scuffle with one rival or another. Frankly, it's considered good for esprit. My honesty, as it turned out, was well exercised. I passed the test and was told to show up the next morning at four a.m. That was when the trucks would come around if they needed mule labor to jump in and roll. I decided maybe my ethics about security work weren't as fastidious as I'd earlier led myself to believe.

A security firm pretty much hired me on the spot because of my service record and probably because I was the closest thing to professional the desk manager had seen in the past six months. He was himself an old vet as well as ex-cop. He could tell I needed money as soon as I could get it, so he put me on the only open shift he had, watching a couple of fire trucks that had to be parked outside overnight while renovations were made to the firehouse bay. They were twelve hour shifts five days a week from eight at night until eight the next morning, paying a little over eight bucks an hour. All those eights lining up seemed to be telling me something worth paying attention to, so I signed on right away and collected my new uniform from the office's wardrobe closet.

I managed to get my old Bronco II running and drove out to the firehouse the next evening. The truck had been sitting idle for most of the past couple years and it tended to overheat if I ran it for too long. Fortunately, I didn't have to drive too far. The job itself was simple. Sit in the truck and be ready to place a phone call with my cell in case anyone started snooping around. It was cool at night and the place was rural, so there was little chance of trouble I couldn't handle. The one consistent enemy in security work is sleepiness and tedium. To stave this off, I started writing, wrestling my laptop around in the slim cab to simulate as comfortable a study as I could. The empty night was perfect. I felt like I'd slipped outside an easy idea of time and imported all my characters with me.

As soon as I claimed a couple of paychecks, I was able to find a place in town to rent with a roommate. I contacted him through Craigslist and went over to tour the apartment and introduce myself. Parker was an affable man in his early fifties with two wildassed dogs, a black boxer named Canaan and an antique and irascible chocolate lab named Cleo. He showed me a small room in the finished basement of the eighty-year-old bungalow. It was tiny but newly refurbished with laminate flooring and had a small private bath attached. Though we would have to share the upstairs kitchen, I had my own private entrance around back. At the end of the tour, Parker somewhat nervously told me that he wanted to make sure I understood that he was gay and that I didn't have a problem with that before committing to a rental agreement. I was surprised he felt the need to say as much, but I answered that was no problem with me if he understood I really liked to drink beer and whiskey. We shook hands and I began moving my few things in that afternoon.

After the firehouse job was finished, the security shifts I got were sporadic and tended to be short term. I tried not to worry about making enough money to keep up with bills while I wrote during the day in the basement room. I had a nice view of the large backyard, a yard that was jungle thick, shading us through the worst of the summer heat. There was a large cicada hatch that year and each afternoon was surrounded with their collective thunder. Ultimately, it made for tolerable company.

I BEGAN seeing my son, Ethan, and had him stay with me whenever he could. Because the room was so small, I bought a folding cot at Walmart and tried to pad it up the best I could with extra bedclothes. We would switch off nights on who had the benefit of the big bed. Ethan has always been remarkably adaptable and stoic. He accepted this arrangement as well as he had all the others, without complaint or disfavor. Even then, I saw the man in him, the complete person that can never escape the dumb pride I feel at being his father. Both of us are quiet people, and we have that odd tension that stoppers words between men who want to share more of themselves with one another than they readily can. But you can feel the effort, the underlying ease, and that sometimes can be a great and true comfort for all the complicated errancy that invades a normal life.

He told me little of what had happened in his life while I was away. He had close friends through his church, a foreign concept to me. I had all I could stand of organized religion when I was a boy and then later when my ex-wife had insisted on attending Sunday services. Then, as well as now, I've felt the fundamental absurdity of believing in a God above your own sense of right and wrong. Archaic dictates seem to have little to do with my idea of good and bad. Still, I knew it wasn't my place to comment on what value he derived from the community he found within the demands of his God. I believe discussing this part of himself made him uncomfortable, perhaps thinking I repudiated this part of him that existed outside of my first-hand knowledge. But even in this reticence, I sensed the force of his personality. I recognized how much was familiar and how much distinct and strong.

It was difficult when I would take him back to his mother's. During that time, they lived in a small upstairs apartment of an old building along a wooded road in West Asheville. There was a Japanese maple in the front yard that burned dramatically with fall colors, leaves softly rattling in the breeze like a chain of paper fans. I walked him up the big wooden halls and watched him go in, saying goodbye but rarely exchanging a hug. When I would go back down and back out to the truck, I felt like the displaced stranger I'd let myself become.

BY THE end of the summer a new security position had come in to work the graveyard shift at the city high school. There had been a recent news report of the building being haunted, so the company had gone through a couple of guards to find one who wasn't superstitious. It promised to be steady employment and offered a private office. My only responsibilities would be to tour the campus every hour and make sure no doors were left unsecured. There would be vast fields of time, a lack of definition I could fill however I chose. There could be no better place to help a book discover what it is supposed to be.

Many events in a writer's life form the elusive quality of voice. But perhaps the elements which seem the slightest may in fact prove the most evenly articulate. The space we inhabit with words is somewhere hard to discuss in plain terms. Overlay and revision are the ways we come to know what matters in our quietest moments. Those long nights were where those moments came to take on meaning for me. The cold halls and the vagrant winds popping at the jambs of unsecured double doors brought truer ghosts than those more easily reckoned. Those Gothic voices became mine. They demanded entry.

Searching for something wise exacts a debt. You can see this in the books of people who live toward their stories. In writing the hurt we take on is part of the larger hurt about the good struggles of strong people. If this is not what we should strive to tell, then what? We are all crossing back and forth, between countries, between shame and dignity, all of us. In this radical life we must find the salvation of what is real, never shying from the severe and strange. That is what writers do if they are honest, what they inflict and grant.

The book was written across those endless nights at the high school. My character, Hiram Tobit, was the best truth I could find, and the book, *Lambs of Men*, was all I have to say about what fathers and sons are to each other. The completeness of that experience is not meant to be flexible nor is it able to change the small troubles of my own life. That is the uncompromising totality of art, the privilege of having created a hypothetical world. I believe the violence poets accomplish is preeminent and necessary, but it cannot be confused with the price that we all pay to understand the hard beauty between who we are and what we say.

Human Animals

—

MY GRANDFATHER had a gift for attracting wild creatures. Rabbits, racoons, squirrels, and possums, abandoned by their littermates, often turned up near the house. He would take them in, nurse and coddle them like house pets. There is a picture of a coon curled around his shoulder like a scarf. He's smiling in a way I can never exactly recall from when he was living.

His eldest sister, Billie, could also call critters to hand. Her specialty was jaybirds. She'd hold a handful of seed and coax them down, though she did complain about getting head pecked a time or two. Still, it never seemed to deter her. She was never as pleased as when she had something living alight in her hands.

After my grandfather's death, my mother and I would sometimes drive to Florida to visit my great-aunt Billie and her husband, Stan. It seemed like an endless journey at the time. All of that piney heat gathering at the shoulders of the interstate became more overwhelming the farther south we went. It seemed to hit its nadir around Valdosta, a placename that was for me then and is still now a mental placeholder for all things "out there," a spot that held no attraction other than having it conclusively in the rearview mirror. Recently, a colleague told me he had interviewed for a teaching position at Valdosta State. Before I had the time to consider what I was doing, I broke friendly protocol and asked if he'd lost his mind. I think I may have offended him, and to be truthful, I've never actually set foot within Valdosta's city limits. It may well be the Paris of south-central Georgia for all I know. But, to this day, the memory of it as a desolate frontier is still something I can't completely shake.

Things did seem to improve a touch once we were over the Florida line. There was a shift in the air, a stir in the foliage. There seemed to be a lot more places where you could buy flip flops, sunglasses, and plaster models of sharks.

We weren't headed to the beach, however. Billie and Stan lived in a small community off the beaten track called Hernando. Their trailer backed up to one of the obscure edges of Tsala Apoka Lake, a moss-dripping incoherence of water that excelled at collecting mosquitoes, alligators, and other murky undesirables. Not the ocean for us. Instead, we were bound for the swamp. Stan had built a boat house years before and enclosed it with aluminum screening. It must have been a fine place to sit at one time, but the timbers had begun to rot to the point that chancing along the deck boards may well have been a risk that offered only a dubious reward. Years later, I'd eat at a ramshackle restaurant teetering over the edge of the Tuckasegee River in Cullowhee, North Carolina, a place comfortably at home in a Cormac McCarthy novel. My girlfriend at the time would refer to the restaurant as that "disheveled wreck about to tumble into the water," and as soon as she said it, I was reminded of Stan's boat house.

The boat house, however, had the added embellishment

of poisonous snakes. They were routinely about, and the fact that this left my great-aunt and great-uncle unperturbed astonished me.

"You don't bother them and they won't bother you," Billie explained.

Even as a boy I understood that snakes were unfairly maligned, but that did little to ease my anxiety when I was outside. Still, as long as I was in the company of Billie and Stan I felt reasonably sure of the order of things.

The days we spent with Billie and Stan were oddly regimented despite the fact that they were both retired and my mother and I were vacationing. It was a household of mornings and evenings. The long, often scorching, middle of the day was left for us to fill on our own.

Billie was up early and always had breakfast on the table before anyone else had crawled out of bed. After we ate and my mother and Billie had their cups of coffee, we adjourned to the Florida room, which was really just the other side of the double wide trailer, though it was the south-facing side and had a long landscape window built in that permitted a steady stream of sunlight even in those early hours. As soon as we settled into our chairs, Billie would pull down her Yahtzee dice, cups, and scoring pads and we would join in what was largely a compulsory ritual. Stan never played with us, and I think Billie refused to let the opportunity to play with someone pass. At the time I was confused by the rules and the strategy of the game, and even today, Yahtzee remains something of a dark art to me. Nevertheless, we played it until the midmorning and the room began to get too hot.

Afternoons were largely spent with Stan in the long concrete garage he'd built years before. It was sealed off on its own and had a pair of window unit air conditioners that blew ice cold. He had a place to work on his cars, though he rarely drove anywhere, preferring to engage in a kind of professional tinkering instead. Mostly, though, he sat in a Lay-Z-Boy with a glass of some of the sweetest tea I've ever tasted and watched a Braves game or a tennis match. If my mother was along, she'd prompt him to tell me stories about the *real* Florida, when he'd first move there in the thirties. He was a good storyteller, and seemed to enjoy the chance to reminisce. But if it was just the two of us, he was content to watch the TV without much talk passing between us. He carried these silences lightly, and I learned a lot about him from that.

The middle of the day was something else altogether. My mother often pulled Billie aside so that they could have time to themselves. I was encouraged to try my hand at fishing if I wanted, but given that such an activity invited a trip to the aforementioned boat house, I typically declined. I could walk the yard and toss the football around, though as hot as it got and with the high probability of slithering playmates, I usually avoided this as well.

Instead, I went to visit Billie's youngest sister, my great-aunt Jeanne. Jeanne lived alone in a small singlewide just down the hill from Billie and Stan's place. Though I didn't know the reference yet, her house was decidedly Havishamish. Everything seemed to remain in deep shadow there, even at noon. She was also in the shade herself. Housebound for years, she had never gone farther than her front porch in the time I'd been around her. I'd learn later that before I was born, she had spent some time institutionalized for some apocryphal mental illness. Since her release, she had lived next door to her sister. When my grandfather was alive, he rarely mentioned her, and only then as "poor Jeanne."

Her sole companion was an irascible chihuahua named Margeaux. She was infamous for her growls and had apparently bitten my grandfather once so hard that he had to be taken to the emergency room for stitches. This was years later, however, and time had blunted her taste for violence even if the capacity was still intact. When I entered, I was greeted with a low growl that didn't so much stop when Jeanne fussed at her but diminished to the point that it was outside the range of human hearing.

We would sit in Jeanne's living room and she would ask a few questions about how I was, how everyone else back in Atlanta was getting along. I was still young enough to be uncomfortable talking with someone so much older and who seemed so remote to me, but I did my best to fill the time. I remember the silences between her questions and my answers were pent, as if whatever I could tell her might solve a problem that extended beyond the simple denotations of what was said. As an adult, when my mother and I had similar conversations under the cloud of her mental illnesses and the medications prescribed to right them, I would recall these long talks with Jeanne and the way that every second passed in her company felt laborious and extractive. When they were over, the sun was brighter, the air more necessary.

That's not to imply that she didn't try her best to be a gracious host. She kept Nilla wafer cookies and always insisted that I take some. When Margeaux saw me partake, she relaxed her unblinking study of me, likely figuring that if I was being offered treats I must share some of the same motivations in the world that she did.

"She's particular about people," Jeanne told me. "It's a good trait."

She leaned over and scooped the tiny animal into her

arms and settled her on her lap. Margeaux's bulging eyes softened and slowly closed into a contented nap. Like Billie and my grandfather, Jeanne's presence alone was enough to solace a creature.

MARGEAUX CAME to expect my visits. This didn't mean she warmed to me exactly, but her growls began to lose some conviction. In turn, I lost some of my nerves as well, and the visits passed a bit more smoothly. Eventually, Jeanne asked if I would like to open a can of dog food and set it on the floor. I wasn't enthusiastic about the idea of doing so but was also too embarrassed to refuse. When I put the dish in front of her, Margeaux looked past her better judgment. She dove right in.

At the time, Jeanne's life seemed, through my boy's eyes, as patently odd, but as I've grown up, I've come to understand how common her predicament was. She simply didn't fit. She was a piece that refused placement. The role of what was impolitely termed as *spinsterhood* ground her down over the years. And yet, she had deep love, reciprocated in its way. She and Margeaux developed real tenderness and understanding between them. By sharing Margeaux with her timid great-nephew, she attempted a bridge of sorts, though I wouldn't understand its importance until many years later. Through all those years of relative isolation, Jeanne had lost the ability to reach out to the world, sealed away by her fundamental difference. Her only window into another heart was through those years holding that ill-tempered chihuahua. By having me feed her, Jeanne wanted me to understand that another creature thought her worth protecting and wanted me to understand that I could be part of an understanding between them. This boy means you no harm. He's kin. And I believe Margeaux trusted Jeanne enough to let me be, whatever trust might mean to a prickly dog with a soft spot for kibble.

I've always been struck when I read Darwin how clear his love for animals was. How he admired them, saw their best qualities as so often beyond the base behavior of his fellow men. I think this is because he chose to see the mind of the animal, to try to understand what meaning they saw in their world. I have no doubt that it is far more complicated than we credit.

Jeanne died years ago, alone, as she was throughout her adult life. Her passing didn't trouble anyone other than her sister, who was herself already widowed by that time. Margeaux had gone about the same time, which was a mercy for them both, I imagine.

When I recently paddled to the edge of a riverbank to study a feeder spring, my attention was diverted to a water strider, a simple insect sometimes referred to as a "Jesus bug" for its ability to walk across the surface of a calm body of water. I have seen them countless times before, but I watched this small creature who normally meant little to me other than as a portion of the great humming truth of the natural world. In the water strider's movements, I detected deliberate care, and though I hesitate to mention it, a decidedly meditative quality that many humans seem to lack in the way they behave themselves in the outdoors. I was drawn to this fellow animal and reminded once more of the multitude of minds that continually surround me and how they must allow some tolerance for one another's inevitable misunderstandings. I wonder what advantage we might find in such mutual grace.

Self-Taught on the Tuck

—

THE KIND of fishing we did when I was a kid usually involved live crickets and a cork, a great deal of sitting in the sun while you waited for something to happen. The electric thrill hit when something took hold of the line and you had your heart in your ears while you tried to play it in, but that was periodic and chancy. When the fish were biting, everyone carried an easy joy, but when the water remained smooth and undimpled, you felt that same liquid heaviness settling into your own blood.

Only when away from the water did I realize what I missed from those fishing trips, even the long profitless ones. This was one of the ironies the Marine Corps taught me, the branch I'd joined to see the world via its oceans. But being posted in Twentynine Palms, California, in the center of the Mojave taught me that water was something you could miss as sharply as if it were a person. Perhaps more.

It would be unjust to dispute the profound beauty of the American desert. Its aesthetics, existing as they do on their own terms, burn away sentimentalism. So much rock and sun and distance make you understand that wilderness is a lot more than a mere word, even if the word is a totem in and of itself. Edward Abbey said wilderness was music, and I get that too. Strange and remote and hypnotic, like lost love.

But while four years in the American desert might teach you respect and a kind of severe admiration, it also bleaches out what is immaterial. A monochromatic world does something to the human eye over time. The green piney life of an outdoor Georgia boyhood can begin to seem like a fairy tale. What matters in the Mojave is line of sight and horizons, True North and back azimuths. Cardinal directions are a great deal more immediate and useful than fables.

When my enlistment expired and I drove back across the country to North Carolina, civilian life was a vertiginous shock. Not only with the pressures of making a new life while balancing young fatherhood and a teetering marriage, but with the literally physical differences of daily life. I was so accustomed to the bland regimen of military order that color itself induced anxiety. It may sound like an exaggeration to say that variety can cause upset, but in my case that was the result. Simply too much of everything happened at once. Everyone seemed to have adjusted to a frequency that to my ears was a persistent, agonizing buzz.

One of the most important books that fell into my hands around that time was Charles Ritz's *A Fly Fisher's Life*. I knew immediately what a rich resource the volume was. It was no dry technical manual. There was narrative life to it. You felt that you came to know Ritz, became comfortable in his company, even if you had to forgive his unabashed use of the exclamation mark. He made you see the art of fishing as something worth pursuing in its own right. And I sorely needed to find a new art.

One day I put down thirty bucks on a Pflueger kit sold by Walmart, another thirty-five on a pair of green rubber waders, but when I got on the water, I realized the set was little better than a toy. The floating line lacked the heft needed to present the fly to the surface of the river. This would have been true even if I had been skilled. And I was not skilled. I had an unerring talent for stranding flies in tree branches or beneath stony ledges. I invented indecipherable knots. Nail scissors became my perpetual companion. It was not the bucolic experience Ritz described along the banks of the Seine, elegantly handling his bamboo rod while trout seemed to rise as a matter of course. Instead, it felt a lot like work. Work that I didn't much like.

That summer, my uncle Buddy drove up from Atlanta to visit. Despite several years of distance, both physical and otherwise, we had been in touch for the last couple of years. He had even flown out to California and visited shortly after my son, Ethan, was born. We'd stood around in the small backyard of fenced-in sand that the corps allotted its married NCOs, smoked awful cigars, and split a gallon of White Russians. He didn't much know what to make of the baby, no more than he did with me.

Back in North Carolina, I could tell he was on firmer ground. The desert had scared him. Like me, he was sensitive to how the land could get inside your head. Put him in the woods with a fishing rod or a long gun in his hand. That, and a whiskey within easy reach, and he could be sociable company for an hour or two. But take him out of a deer camp for too long and you soon understood why he'd run afoul of so many former hunting buddies. He attacked every kindness anyone would try to do for him, beat back friendship like it might be fatally contagious. Ultimately, I think he simply couldn't come to terms—as many of us can't—with the fact that his life had become an obvious counterfeit of what he had expected it to be.

It was my birthday when he came up, my twenty-fourth. By now, Ethan was running around and talking, bigheaded and convivial as three-year-olds are. We sat discussing how much he'd grown for as long as the conversation could circle before Buddy said he wanted me to step outside and see something. I went with him, a knowing tightness in my chest. Since I was a boy, he had liked to make grand gestures in front of others, playing the big man to an audience. Out of habit, I tolerated it; my own resentment embarrassed me.

He lifted an Orvis rod and reel from his car trunk. He pieced the rod together, stripped line and threaded it through the guides. He was as inexperienced with fly casting as I was, but this wouldn't prevent his own authority in the moment. I was used to this kind of submissive patience, though each time the bright orange line bellied, coiled, and shot forward, it was harder to find something to do with my hands. Finally, he gave it to me, and I held a true fly rod for the first time.

Anyone who has ever taken a well-made fly rod to hand knows the particular grace of the object. It is as unlike a spinner rod as a clapboard church is to a basilica. The long aerial-like extension of the rod tip might as well be a sportsman's calligraphic brush. Even with an amateur's degree of skill, you can achieve beauty. It's easy to become intoxicated by the simple metrics of the cast, which is why so many green fishermen struggle to land fish when they take these exquisite instruments down to the water. They are stunned by the experience of the cast in the same way you can be stunned by a piece of classical sculpture. You're in love with something that is designed to exceed your reach. And so, the fly is in the air a great deal more than it should be, which is no way to catch fish.

Many rookies make the argument that catching fish isn't

the most important concern at the riverside. That there are nobler sentiments in being gripped by the rhythm of the water: to sight migratory birds or discover botanic wonders along the bank, for instance. While these may be nobler arguments, they are still wrong. Casting is cinematic, easy to admire for its grandeur and spectacle, but it isn't a profound and intimate shock of reaching into a different world. It doesn't freeze time. Fighting a fish connects you to a place without regard for your success. It is a *becoming*.

Still, I now had a rod worthy of my ambition, and I began to train myself in the backyard of my apartment. I worked on the single haul, the double haul, and the all-important roll cast. I studied sketches of mending line and tried to imagine a shedding current in the tall grass. Within a couple of weeks, the rod began to feel natural in my hand. While I practiced, Ethan came out with his Mickey Mouse fishing set, and so we'd spend an hour or two together before going back into the house.

All through that summer, while my son and I improved our casts, life at home got worse. I'd been married to Ethan's mother when I was nineteen and she was twenty-six. In the years since, resentment had grown from feeding on itself. Family on both sides had warned against the age difference, the contrary temperaments, the general wrongness of the thing itself, but the more reasonable the criticism we heard, the more determined we became to defy it. This stubbornness on my part began to erode a couple of years after we married when I'd picked up Raymond Carver's collected stories for the first time. Reading them and their record of so many fractured domestic lives was like reading a secret history of my own unhappiness.

Still, his mother and I managed our days by living through Ethan, despite the fact that anger was always a centimeter beneath the surface. All you had to do was scratch and watch it turn red.

So I worked, attended college, and fished. When I got home, Ethan was often in bed or close to it. If he was still awake, I would go in and read and talk to him before he went to sleep. We talked about when he was a little bigger he would be allowed to come along with me to the river.

My practice began paying off. I drove the riverside road to see where the other fly fishermen had settled in along the Tuckaseegee. I nudged my truck into the narrow parking spaces along the shoulder and waded in, ensuring respectful distance from the others who had already begun to cast. I began to read riffles and to place the fly so that it glided past active pools. That other world had begun to reach out and shape me.

When I wasn't fishing or reading for school, I had gone back to my Raymond Carver collection. There was one story in the volume, a fishing story, that had begun to mean something new. "So Much Water, So Close to Home" is an unsettling look at the buried emotional violence in a faltering marriage. Told by the wife, Claire, it relates the aftermath of a murder and its discovery when her husband and a group of his fishing buddies find the body of a young woman in the Naches River. Though the bare facts of the story are horrifying in and of themselves, the true focus is the way seemingly decent people behave when no one is looking. The husband, Stuart, seems to recognize the moral line he and his friends crossed when they decided to stay and fish for the weekend even after finding the young woman's body snagged in the river. However, he makes feeble attempts to justify his actions.

Rereading the story, I was struck by my false memory of it. I remembered the point-of-view being that of Stuart and how the narrative ended with his wife's disgust at his callous treatment of the body. What I read anew was far more distressing. Through Claire's voice we see Stuart as simply another practitioner of idle cruelty that is the rule in a woman's life rather than the exception. She imagines herself as the murder victim, sees threats distant as well as intimate.

I thought a great deal about all that. About how I was fishing in the river with something dead hidden beneath the surface. The fact had been plain for some time, but now it became abrasive. The performance that had been going on at home was exhausting Ethan's mother and me, even if we refused to admit it. The petty arguments and manipulations were inept and self-defeating efforts to gain leverage over each other. The discrete world I'd felt pulling back on the other end of the fishing line wasn't only nature reminding me of what it was on its own terms; it was a chance to teach myself who I was. It was a chance to become a responsible father. I knew that staying in a bad marriage was seductive because it would let things appear to settle, to simply go on. But to stay in would be untrue to Ethan, and to her, and to the better man I wanted to be. There might be something living down in the water too, not just that deathly shame. Something that could be a faithful example to my child, even if it meant causing sharp hurt before things could get better. That's what I hoped, at least.

At the end of the summer, my uncle Buddy drove up to fish with Ethan and me. We checked the dam release tables to make sure we would have a few hours before the water would rise high enough that we'd be driven back to the bank. He had bought his own fly-fishing rig and was eager to test it on the river. Ethan still wasn't big enough to fish, but a few weeks before he'd gotten a toy fish net, and he was determined to take it down to the Tuck, even if it meant watching our casts from the safety of big rocks.

We got out early and had sporadic luck in some of the upper holes. But by lunchtime we'd moved twice and still only landed a couple of small rainbows apiece. I suggested we try one more spot to fish hard before the dam release would take effect, a wide stretch of shoal water across from the water treatment plant. I made no promises, but I knew the fish were consistently active through there. This was where I'd show my uncle what I'd learned, how I'd spent all this time with myself to good use. And I wanted Ethan to see it too. I wanted him to realize I had a sense of what I was doing. Maybe if he saw that click into place other things might as well.

I led Ethan by his free hand into water that came to his waist. With the other he held his net, which he dragged across the river's surface as we went. He giggled at the current swirling around him, and I did too.

Buddy went downstream and began casting at the end of the tear drop island. It was pretty out there, he shouted back. Reminded him of the Rappahannock. It was a river that meant nothing to me other than a place on a map, but I could tell he intended it as a compliment. For a man who was stingy in direct praise, I was satisfied with what he had to say.

I found Ethan a big rock that lent a good vantage, told him to stick to it and waded a dozen yards toward a swift run. The crash of water flung a pleasant spray so that it was cool and comfortable even in the full sun. I had a pair of nymphs tied on and I deliberately stripped line and cast, watched the floating line switch and cock in the air. Glancing back at Ethan, I could see he was as taken by the rhythmic spell as I was. Then I shot the line and

watched the leader quarter through the fast water and jostle
downstream.

Within minutes, I began to tear into them. It's like that
sometimes, becomes impossible to miss a single fish. You
expect the line to go tight as soon as you complete the cast,
and it does. These were good fighting trout. Eleven or twelve
inches. Not record breakers but as pure a fish as you could
hope. Buddy could see the success I was having. I noticed
him discreetly creeping closer. Soon, he was into them as
well. His rod bowed and jerked and did so again nearly as
soon as he released each new trout. We kept on. Time slid.

The water began to rise. The dam release had shuttled
its way downstream. At first, it was only a gentle difference, but soon it became much more. The water was to my
waist and coming up fast. Reluctantly, I realized we needed
to head back to the bank. I turned my head to tell Ethan we
needed to pack it in, but he was gone.

Every parent knows that panic. When the child is
missing. If you want to know the pain of an animal crying,
pack that into a moment and you have it.

His head popped up. He had dropped his net and gone
into the current after it. He was chin deep and still chasing
the long handle. I shouted to him, told him to be still. I
don't believe he heard me. All he had in mind was what
the river had stolen from him. I got to him faster than I'd
believed possible and pulled him to my chest. Only then did
he realize what had happened and I could feel him shiver
against me. He did so all the way back to the bank.

We collapsed and held tight to each other while that river
just rolled. I held him and myself still as long as I could.

Those Boys

—

IN 2015, my friend Mark and I talked about going down to Cayo Costa, but I really didn't see a way to make it work. My wife, April, and I were in a new city and a new house, and the island was a lot closer for Mark, who taught at a private university in northern Florida. So, it was a casual point of discussion going into the fall, this chance to get down to the Gulf Coast in the bad end of December. A point of discussion, but not much else.

In October I got a call from the police department in Asheville, North Carolina, telling me that my eighteen-year-old son, Ethan, was dead by his own hand. All I could do was give the phone to April while I went to my study to drink whiskey and rave.

I didn't know that while I locked myself away with these new and hungry demons that April had already called Mark and told him to come see me because she knew he was the closest thing I had to a brother. The next day he was on a plane.

Mark is a writer, and he's known as one of the friendliest and most decent members of that dubious community. At more than one writers' retreat when he was out of earshot, I've heard women and men both exclaim about his being the best-looking writer in Appalachia (admittedly, a low bar). If he would have served in the Marines instead of going through the Citadel, we would have called him a poster-boy Marine—big, athletic, and gleaming with unassuming moral virtue—the kind of guy that would have been sweet candy for a recruiter. All that would be insufferable if it were a pose, but these qualities are so natural to him that they cannot be denied, even by those with a contrary turn of mind. This is all to say, the only thing you really need to know about him is that he's the kind of man that gets a phone call about a friend's dead son and the next day he's on a plane.

When he landed, he came into my study to listen to me for three days. We sat, talked about books, just about anything that got me through. It was hard to see him go.

I went back to teaching within a week. It wasn't stoic. It was simply the only way I knew to put one tired foot in front of the other. A couple of weeks later, April told me that her parents wanted to buy a plane ticket so I could go down with Mark to spend some time in the Gulf, catch some red fish, and eat well. They wanted me to have some-thing to pull toward, I think; they knew that if I didn't, there would be little left in the world that would ever matter to me again. Once I'd tied up the endless semester, I flew down directly to the Sandford airport in Orlando, exchang-ing the cold rain of Knoxville for the absurd Florida heat. Mark and his little boy Silas greeted me. It was good to see them both. It felt like coming back to family.

IN THOSE days, there was such numbness. I would be in the car and suddenly have to pull to the side of the road when the magnitude of grief attacked me. I learned that the only way to get through a day was to ignore the mind and live in my body as much as possible, to see the world only in material terms. I wasn't forgetting Ethan; instead, I was trying to teach myself to live without knowledge of any other path but the one I was on. I needed things to be fine and simple and full of sunlight.

The drive down the coast was wonderful for that. The last fifteen miles of highway before reaching the ferry, we began to see the osprey nests. Silas, seven-year-old Silas, with his encyclopedic knowledge of anything that flew and his especially fanatical enthusiasm for raptors, bobbed in his seat.

"There's another one!" he said, pointed. "Look at that sucker!"

I agreed that it was incredible, the heaping basket of sticks arranged intricately atop the telephone poles. Though I'd spent years in the Georgia woods as a boy, I'd never seen such an impressive nest, and here they were, appearing every few hundred yards. I hadn't yet seen one of the birds, but if that roost was anything to judge them by, I knew they would have to be spectacular to see on the wing.

A while later the highway petered out into a trail of crushed shell and we coasted into a quiet cove where we found the outfitting house and the ferry dock. Silas and I started moving gear from the back of the car down to the dock while Mark went inside to check about passage to the island. We had three coolers of supplies. We meant to live well while we were out there. It turned out that we had plenty of time to wait. The ferry was a sixteen-foot covered boat with rickety twin outboards and could only carry half a dozen people at a time. The next round was already full, so we settled in and got comfortable. Mark wandered off to look at some of the coastal mansions on the opposite bank while Silas and I fiddled with the fishing tackle. It was awfully warm where we were, but the island breeze lent the spot a particular gentleness.

A few minutes later a middle-aged couple pulled into the lot in a factory-fresh BMW and toted their Eddie Bauer bags down and set them under a shade tree, just a few feet from us. The husband had gone inside to check in. The wife, pointedly ignoring us, strode to the water's edge and surveyed Pine Island Sound. From the mangroves across the way, a great bird left its roost and rose enormously.

"Now, I wonder what kind of bird that is," she wondered aloud.

"Why, that's an osprey!" Silas shouted as he popped to his feet. Before she could recover from the shock of having her train of thought hijacked, Silas launched into a hip pocket TED talk on osprey migration and nesting patterns. This soon gave way to a generalized lesson on ornithological identification in both fledgling and adult specimens. Like any emphatic educator, his hands jabbed and sawed the air when he included some telling point. If he sensed the student didn't follow, the gesticulations grew more rapid and pugilistic. After a few minutes, I feared it was time to cut things short before he did damage to this slow learner.

"Birds are important to him," I explained.

Wide-eyed, she nodded as she gained several yards of breathing room. When it was time to board for the trip out, she and her husband settled in the stern, putting themselves as discreetly out of the way as they could.

The big outboards coughed and we could feel it in the soles of our shoes. As soon as the boat swung around the headland, the engines opened up and we bounced across the hard flat blue. I had to clap my hand on my head to keep my cap in place. It was the fastest ferry I've ever been on. I glanced back at the pilot in his board shorts and fishing shirt open at the throat. He had the island grunge of a young Kurt Russell in *Overboard* made more piratical by a wind-snapped purple bandanna cinched around his neck . He didn't smoke, but he looked like the kind of man who would be comfortable with a cigar propped against his lower lip. All in all, he seemed like he knew what he was doing, so I settled back and watched as we overtook the sea, pleased to be down here with the birds and the wind at the edge of America.

THE DOCK at Cayo Costa was even quieter than where we'd left at Pine Island. As a Florida state park, it clearly ran on a shoestring budget. There wasn't even anyone on duty to collect camping fees, just a box with envelopes where you paid the two-dollar-a-night fee and tore a validation stub to take with you. The only other permanent-looking structure was a small general store advertising live bait. On the porch, somebody's, maybe the storekeeper's, brindle boxer yawned and grinned as we settled our camping things in a teetering pile next to the wagon-hitched four wheelers that would take us to the other side of the island. Whenever one of the drivers turned up, that is.

Mark and Silas went into the store to get some bait and see if they could get in touch with a driver. I walked over to the tree line and gazed down several of the intersecting foot paths, inviting throughways of blond sand. In the shade the overall quietness was remarkable, even meditative. Simple trips to the beach have never held that much appeal to me. For me, the seaside experience largely consists of sunburn and relentless glare, deprived of anything constructive to occupy the time. It's a place of headaches and faint nausea. I'm convinced that it's no accident that in Camus's *The Stranger*, Mersault commits murder on a beach. But here, along the paths, I glimpsed a rich interiority at odds with what I had come to expect. I could feel the press of the Gulf beyond, the looming fact of that great power intensifying the immediate silence. Walking along those trails was like stepping within immense, praying hands.

Mark and Silas came out with plastic bags of frozen squid and told me the storekeeper had radioed for the man who drove the four wheelers. I took one of the bags of thawing squid and massaged it between my thumb and forefinger. Already, it was beginning to stink.

"He give any fishing advice?" I asked.

Mark shrugged, said, "He told me to throw it in the water. Wait till the fish bite."

Classic. A wise man or a wise guy one.

We didn't have to wait long before the driver turned up and helped us load the wagon. He drove us past a grove of palm trees and then we entered a forest of mixed undergrowth, the worn path soft in the deep bends from the traffic of fat tires. Occasional breaks in the canopy revealed the formidable osprey nests in the tops of big cypress trees. A branch with a view, for sure.

The driver pulled onto a patch of flattened cordgrass and cut the engine, pointed up a foot trail. Apparently, we were on our own from here on out. Silas and I unloaded and walked everything the rest of the way to the campsite while Mark tipped the driver. Some hundred feet later we found a gentle sandy opening guarded on three sides by a tight wall of buttonwood. The sounds of the sea were a persistent whisper just the other side of the barrier. We all decided that we couldn't have had better luck. We quickly pitched camp then took our chairs and fishing tackle down to the beach.

The water rolled pleasantly under a steady offshore breeze. A big marlin broke the sea several hundred yards out. Ripped the surface five or six times. Though it was only something to gawp at, it made the process of baiting our hooks for the surf a bit more freighted. If you had any doubt that this was good fishing water, there was the proof. Failure could only be a matter of bad luck or your own elaborate incompetence.

Despite the advice Mark had gotten at the general store, I was sure that there had to be more to catching red fish than simply letting the squid sink to the bottom, so I began a slow retrieval, bringing the concealed hook back like I would a simple crank bait back on a Tennessee lake. I threw in the occasional variation, tried different depths, twitched the rod tip from time to time, but neither Mark nor I got the first bite. The only thing we'd attracted were a few gulls passing curiously close. That and a couple of figures approaching from the bend of the shoreline, the only people we could see on that section of beach. We still had plenty of daylight, so we settled back to watch the water.

"Dad, why is that lady naked?" Silas said, squinting.

The pair, a not very young couple, had drawn close enough to become bracingly visual. A moment later I realized it was the man and his wife from the ferry.

"Cover your eyes, son," Mark quickly told him.

I likewise heeded this advice. When I looked again, the couple had turned back and gone the other way. Apparently, they were as averse to our company as we were to theirs. Fine, let them have that side of the island. We were suitably comfortable with the alligators over here.

"Why don't we try the fish again," I suggested. I believe we were all grateful for the chance to redirect our attention.

We walked a little further into the surf and began casting again. When we did, the gulls came back, tilting sharply at the surface of the water.

"Look at those shearwaters!" Silas admired.

And that's exactly what I was doing, watching the bird as it swung up and bounced on a thermal—aloft, expectant— a moment before it collapsed its wings and shot toward the sea.

"Oh no."

I realized what he was after, but as I jerked the rod back and cranked the reel to get clear I felt the sickening tug at the other end of the line. The gull rose, flew fast and low like it meant to pin itself to the sunset. But then the line went taut, the gull's head snapping back from the hook buried in its beak.

"It's caught! The shearwater's caught!" Silas cried.

Mark and I exchanged a look.

"Reel it in," he told me.

Reluctantly, I did. I tried to be as steady as possible, hoping that the bird would fly closer, but now it was panicked and had no sense of direction. Instead, it thrashed and yanked in a vain effort to free itself. Over my shoulder, I heard Silas making sad, murmuring sounds. Eventually, I brought the gull in as gently as possible for the final few yards. Mark grabbed and held the bird close to his body to calm it, prying its beak open while I put down the rod and tried to work the hook out, but the barb wouldn't pass.

"Silas!" I shouted.

I needed him to get the knife from the tackle box. When I glanced behind me, I saw him on his knees, hands clasped, praying for the gull.

"Silas!"

He lifted his grimacing face.

"Yes, sir?"

"The knife, buddy. Grab the knife."

He jumped to his feet, eager to have some role in the

rescue. He rummaged through the plastic compartments, found the Case knife, and opened it for me. I cut the line and pushed the hook through. Mark set the gull down. It staggered a few steps before it realized the hook was no longer in its beak and it flew for the safety of the island interior.

"Guys," Silas said after a few moments had passed. "Maybe we shouldn't fish anymore this afternoon."

"I think that's a good idea, son."

"I'm just going to go look at some osprey nests, okay?"

Mark agreed that was a good idea. Once Silas wandered off toward the tree line, Mark pulled a thermos of chilled whiskey from the cooler. It was every bit as good as it sounds. We were content to merely watch the water roll for a half hour or more, wait for the sun to flatten itself against the sea. A good drink at the right time is not to be underestimated. In a while, the embarrassment with the gull was behind us. We had this spread of solitary beach and the evening campfire to come. We were well off. We were expansive.

"Check out this guy," Mark said, gesturing at a man walking the waterline. Over his shoulder he carried a brace of red fish. When he got close enough, Mark asked him how he managed to catch them.

"Awww, there's nothing to it," he said. "Just throw it in the water. Wait till the fish bite."

Learning a Place
by Its Waters

———

WE PUT in on the Holston River beneath a bridge on Asheville Highway. It's Sunday morning and still warm despite being late October. The boat, an Old Town Saranac canoe, has only touched the water once before. That was yesterday with my wife, April. On that outing, fish ripped the surface like it accused them of grievous acts. Today is my stepson Iain's turn and there is a calmer air. I see only the occasional ring of some soft aquatic nuzzle. As we wade out and the canoe settles into the river, a tractor trailer rolls across the bridge overhead, bucks the substructure so that it sounds like the whole span could come down on our heads. It's an odd start to the placid day on the water I had planned. Knoxville is still growing its way around us, though it's been more than four years since we moved here. This place, it seems, is a slow vine.

Still, the balance on the water is familiar. Even before the first paddle stroke, there is that tug and give that means the boat is fitted to its natural state. I know it well and welcome the change, but Iain is nervy in that young teenage way. He's always had dizzy energy, and in the boat that anxiety is as obvious as a handshake. We rock too much for such a broad-beamed canoe, but when I tell him to settle he does, and before long we are slotted to the waterway. We simply glide.

Like so many Americans, my wife and I moved for work. That's what Knoxville was for us after living in western North Carolina for many years. A move of necessity. It's hard, though not uncommon, to shift homes when you're on the verge of middle age. Hard too if you're an adolescent. But the effort was collective, and we settled into an old stone cottage to make something familiar out of what seemed strange at the outset. I think it helps a great deal that there's a river within easy driving distance of our front door. I like the idea of being able to step off into something that is in perpetual circulation.

Iain's adjustment to this place has been by degrees. He was raised in Asheville, where liberal politics and a more generally permissive culture are largely a matter of course. Knoxville intimidated him at first, I believe. It's a conservative town, and the kids don't preen under the undivided attention of income-secure parents. They're made with thicker armor. But he's learned to hammer together his own version. After Ethan's death, he had to plug himself into a new role, as we all did. He's shed some of his nerves, though he sometimes needs to be reminded to slow down and take things in. The river has proven the ideal place for that. It's a way for us to let time and memory carry us and think about what things were like once and what they are now.

Moving water has a distinct hold over my imagination. When I grew up hunting and fishing the middle Georgia woods, still or stately water was the rule. Brown and slow. Often small ponds that held pan and catfish. If there were rivers, they had gone a deep ochre from rubbing up against deep cut clay banks. If a river was a metaphor for the passage of time, then a middle Georgia river was a vehicle for the past perpetually revisited.

But my experience as an adult on Appalachian streams was something entirely different. In the mountains, water didn't merely flow, it *coursed*. When you happened to be on a boat headed downstream, it introduced a set of urgent controversies that needed to be solved quickly. The high-country rivers speak a different idiom. They make you pay attention.

Shadows cross over us as we come under the boughs that sport incendiary color. But the wooded surroundings soon give way to river-facing lots. Ranch homes built in on obscure-seeming roads become increasingly regular, dispelling any sense of wilderness. Small docks with bass boats are continuous along this stretch, though we're still early enough in the day to avoid their disturbance. Once we get to the confluence, that luxury will likely be forfeited. All deep channel and horsepower. But now we pass through a serene suburb, the homes growing larger as we cross the line into the Holston Hills district. The big three-story homes stare across the clubhouse fairway while a small figure tries to chip his way out of a bunker.

One of my favorite passages of writing about rivers is in Mark Twain's *Life on the Mississippi*. In it, he talks about how learning to navigate the Mississippi as a steamboat pilot prepared him for many of the great challenges he would later face in life. The colors and shapes of currents became a kind of semiology that he would later translate into his own work as a writer. Like Twain, I believe in the advantages of reading the natural world like it's a book. We give away a lot when we fail to consider the fact that a great many things in the woods and on the water don't readily cede to our first impressions of them. And I can think of no better way to read a place than from the standpoint of its waterways.

Knoxville is remarkably gifted in its allotment of moving water. The Tennessee River begins here where the Holston and French Broad converge, which means it's a river with ancestors in two states. The Holston traces its three forks all the way back to the knobby southwest corner of Virginia, while the French Broad—the contrary French Broad—fights its way west from Transylvania County, North Carolina, across the Great Smoky Mountains before it finds its placid groove along the green belly of east Tennessee before evolving into one of the great rivers of the eastern United States. It's a pretty river, despite how many times it's been dammed and changed into something it wasn't. There's a lot of power in that water. A lot of money too. Just ask the TVA.

Cormac McCarthy wrote memorably about the Tennessee River in what may arguably be *the* great Appalachian novel, *Suttree*. He sets a very particular tone when he describes the river's

> alluvial harbored bones and dread waste, a wrack of cratewood and condoms and fruitrinds. Old tins and jars and ruined household artifacts that rear from the fecal mire of the flats like landmarks in the trackless vales of dementia praecox.

A far cry from a tourism pitch. And while it's true that McCarthy was merging the inner landscape of his doomed protagonist with his troubled fate, McCarthy was also detailing the river as it was during the middle of the twentieth century. A waterway that bore the consequences of industry before the arrival of the Clean Water Act.

Something merely commercial, not much different than an extended production line.

That's changed over the years. Like many cities, Knoxville has recognized the value of an attractive waterfront. A system of greenways winds its way through much of the downtown and as far as the suburbs. They've even managed to turn Suttree himself into a recreational draw. My favorite take out in town is a manicured strip of public park complete with a floating dock made available for general use. There are picnic tables and a couple of microbreweries within walking distance. It's called Suttree Landing, a fact I'm sure would cause McCarthy no small degree of amusement.

Here, on the lower Holston, things enjoy a vestige of the sylvan before they meet the harder modernity of the Tennessee. The water splits at Boyd Island. If we were to bear left toward the main branch, we would continue along a similar course, passing over French Broad Shoals where a creek feeds a pleasant riffle into the stream. Instead, we steer for the narrow gut to the right where we have only a couple of canoe lengths from one bank to the other. This is the first time I've needed to mind my J stroke in order to keep us moving straight ahead with little room for error. The foliage crowds in so close here that a moment's inattention would have us running up under tree limbs, which might not be dangerous necessarily but would still damage any points we might be able to tally for the sake of style.

Soon, though, we're through that constriction as the right bank opens up into a large field crowded with several hundred people. We've unwittingly strayed into a major sporting event, though it isn't one that would be covered by local media. A migrant community of Central American workers are rooting for their soccer teams dressed out in professional-looking uniforms of vivid blue and electric yellow. The players deftly pass the ball and look for the suggestion of weakness in the defenders. As we pass quietly by, it's hard not to feel like we've eavesdropped. As we round the next turn and slip back into the woods, we hear the thud of a swift kick and the roar of triumphant Spanish as someone has managed to score a goal.

I recognize how lucky we are to see the community like this. Most travelers' impressions of Knoxville are gathered at a far more rapid pace than what can be got by paddle and current. It's all interstate and access roads. With I-40 and I-75 intersecting here, freight runs through one axis or the other any hour of the day, any day of the week, so tight and quick traffic is to be expected. The city's more general layout is a longitudinal affair, east to west, old to new. Over the years, everything has developed in a predictable line that chases the setting sun. Along I-40 the homes shed decades and gain acreage. Distinct architectural lines gradually succumb to geometric reduction, so that it's easy to see that the nickname for these westernmost "Knox boxes" is well earned.

For my first few years in Knoxville, the rush hour road is how I got a feel for the town. I often volunteer to teach the earliest classes offered at the community college where I work to get the regimented parts of the day done. I've never thought time is something that should feel like a straitjacket. Driving across town is part of that restricted experience, that sense of confinement. Once that's done and the classes have had a chance to hit their marks, I can sit and think about writing and reading and how to make those things take hold in my students. It's not the kind of work that easily segments itself according to the clock. And that's exactly the point as far as I'm concerned.

Given my dislike of keeping a fixed schedule, I recognize how this repeated back and forth has prejudiced my view of the city. It's largely become just something that needs to be gotten out of the way, a trip between here and there. But the river offers something else. Taking to the water breaks the stranglehold of contemporary living. When I decide to travel by canoe, it is a way to see my home in a different light. It does the important magic of disturbing time by extending space.

Urban paddling is, however, a significant compromise for most boaters. Many of us that have an affinity for rivers have cultivated that love by being in green places. Stone bluffs and wooded ridgelines make for better bird watching than marble quarries and barge moorings.

But there's something thrilling too about rounding a curve in the river and seeing a P-51 Mustang roar overhead as it takes off from the Knoxville Downtown Island Airport. I point out the distinct fuselage of the World War II fighter to Iain and explain its role against the Luftwaffe. I'm not sure if the plane belongs to a wealthy enthusiast or is part of some air show, whether it is a replica or a restored original. A minute later we spot a B-17 bomber lumbering its way toward us as it comes in to land, and we have a pretty good idea that there must be an event in the area. As a kid, I was a sucker for old reruns like *Victory at Sea* that featured cockpit footage of American fighter pilots in action. Before I realize what I'm doing, I've launched into a five-minute lecture on the various strengths and weaknesses of the planes the disputing nations flew against one another. A sly smile crosses Iain's lips.

The excitement in my voice is all too obvious. Doubtless, Iain has picked up on my contradicting myself from a few minutes earlier when I griped about every speedboat that tore past us without regard for the rocking wakes we'd had to canoe through. I'd said only a redneck sonofabitch would prefer a motor over a paddle, and here I was prattling on about the weird grace built by Grumman. While he keeps grinning, I tell him to turn around and mind his stroke. I square my sense of inconsistency with my admiration of Twain. He could appreciate the natural magnitude of the Mississippi while still thrilling to the throb of a steam engine that shuddered the deck beneath his feet.

We paddle back across the channel as quickly as we can, wary of being caught too close to the middle when another speed jockey may decide to thunder by. I know that the back end of the island, despite the busy airplane traffic, is known to harbor raptors, so I want to put us close to the bank. Almost as the thought strikes me, we catch sight of an osprey flying no more than a dozen feet over the river. Nature's fighter pilot doing what it was meant to do. We wait to see if it strikes a fish, but it speeds on, disappearing into the afternoon glare of sun against the downtown skyline.

We come to the take out half an hour later. By now it's hot and we're grateful to be off the water and securing the canoe to the roof rack. We only brought along snacks, and a McDonald's hamburger sounds like a likely remedy. Our backs are sore. We have the slight flush of sunburn. Tomorrow is Monday, after all, so we should settle ourselves into the habitual groove and begin to think about how to make ourselves part of the weekly rush. Still, any time we see a raptor, I consider the day a success. To see that uncommon yet contained ferocity on the wing reminds me that we live beneath a sky of stark wonders.

Under Weight

—

IT WAS my first backpacking trip in years, and we were up on Roan Mountain in late September. My friend Mark and his son Silas were meeting my stepson Iain and me at the hostel where it was all supposed to end. We arrived early for the shuttle that would take us to the top, so we stood around in the seasonably warm sun, catching up and hefting one another's packs to get an idea of what we were toting. Silas was still just eleven, so his backpack was not much different than you'd expect to see. Tidy, trim, and light. I'd slapped together an ad hoc rig for Iain. A big pack that my wife had used when she skied out west, fitted with a bulky Coleman sleeping bag, and an old military surplus sleeping pad tied to the outside. Mark and I both carried old external frame backpacks, which were still fashionable twenty years earlier, but once you looked around and saw the slick, ultralight gear that the other trail bums at the hostel were wearing, I started to suspect we looked a lot like what we were: two middle-aged amateurs about to get our asses handed to them.

The recognition provoked a sick feeling in my stomach. When I packed the night before, I'd been thinking of what it meant to be on a forced march in the Marine Corps. There, a heavy pack was a right and responsibility. You weighted the pack for the sake of conditioning. A prescribed burden that had nothing to do with practicality. Instead, you wanted the strain and suffering. And that was before the helmet, flak jacket, and rifle were added to the mix. That was what a Marine was, after all—a vessel for hardship. But that version of me was a long time gone. As soon as I turned the pack up and let it fall onto my shoulders, I knew the weight I was carrying was twice what I could bear. I thought to see if there was anything I might quickly subtract and take back to the car, but before I could, the shuttle showed up.

We rode up to Carvers Gap in the back of a limousine because it was only the four of us going that time of day and the driver didn't want to bother pulling the bus around. He was gruff mannered and would later get his name in a national outdoor publication for refusing to shut down shuttle operations or his hostel during the spring 2020 Covid-19 quarantine. Got his name in the paper, and not in a good way, as my wife would say. He had cranked up some blend of New Country crap that advertised patriotism and a penchant for good times at the lake with cheap beer, those qualities being putatively entwined. Mark and I traded smirks while we rode to the top without saying much.

At the trailhead, we thanked him for the ride and shouldered our kits, crossed the road and stepped onto the path. In his essay "Walking," Thoreau talks about the intuitive relationship between walking and thinking. Of course, he preferred to strike out on an independent course, avoiding anything as pedestrian as a determined trail. He would likely have doubted the quality of any thinking that might occur on a world-famous trail trod by untold millions across the years. But even if we follow a physical rut, I disagree that we must by force follow a mental one. Our experiences, by their very nature, diverge daily, in both small and large ways. I had become sharply aware of this in the four years since my son, Ethan, died. In a way, I needed a posted trail to follow, a way to find a course of footsteps I should have followed as a younger man.

Being a stepparent is surely one of the most thankless roles a person can take on, perhaps exceeded only by being a stepchild. Despite the effort and love you invest as a stepparent, it's always going to be somewhat of a substitute. There are a couple of ways of going at this. First, you can try to ignore the circumstances and claim no distinction between blood and kinship. We are part of the same tribe, this theory affirms, and that is the bond that matters at root. You are my son, and I am Dad. It's true that this works in many families, though it seems more likely to succeed when the birth parent is largely uninvolved in the child's life. The second approach, the one Iain and I have tacitly embraced, recognizes the unique quality of the relationship, that other people who might get their feelings hurt are involved, namely his natural father. When talking to others about him, I normally preface it with "my stepson" or, if I'm trying not to get too bogged down in details, "the kid." That way you avoid the puzzled looks when someone asks where he is for the weekend and you tell him he's spending some time with his dad. Iain, for his part, always calls me by my first name. It's a preference that's always seemed reasonable enough to me.

Despite the family politics, Iain and I share a few things that are discretely ours: horror movies, sushi, and the more rugged aspects of an outdoor life, particularly canoeing and hiking. I'm sometimes surprised by how willing he is to go along on these treks. I suspect he likes that they provide a

way for us to be in each other's company without the added
freight of having to work out the reason we've chosen to
have some time alone. Also, it's easier to relax in the woods,
to drop the burden of the parts each of us feels compelled
to play at home. I sometimes wonder if this way of being is
what life may look like when he's my age and I've become
an old man.

Thirty minutes in and I already knew I was in trouble.
Day trips out along this stretch of trail were wholly unlike
what currently bore down on my shoulders. Foolishly, I'd
come out without trekking poles, so every time I leaned
forward into the grade, the more pressure I felt grinding into
my lower back. The boys were now well ahead, and I could
tell Mark was holding back at my pace for the sake of cama-
raderie. He'd kept himself in excellent shape, even though
we had grudgingly admitted to each other we were defini-
tively across the Rubicon of middle age. Far enough across
that our feet weren't even wet anymore, I'd said. We crested
the ridge and on level ground I began to bear up better. Not
good, but better. I tightened up on the straps to try to get
the center of gravity as high as I could. When I did, I could
hear the whole big bottle of Bulleit bourbon slosh. More
weight I didn't need. I drew on a piece of military wisdom.
Each step planted was one closer to being done.

Finally the trail leveled and we came up into the bald.
At the peak, a cluster of boulders loomed. We dropped our
packs and clambered to the top of the formation to get the
view that many Appalachian Trail thru-hikers claim is one
of their favorite horizons throughout the entire Georgia to
Maine trek. With the sun suspended over such an imperial
landscape, it's easy to take them at their word.

After a few minutes of admiring our surroundings, we
scouted for a place to pitch our tents. Mark assured me that

the best places would go quickly because we were still in range of campers who would only hike in the three miles from the gap. Glorified car campers, Mark called them. Our plan was to overnight here on the bald then do about ten miles the next morning and spend a second night on the sheltered back end of Hump Mountain. Nothing too strenuous, especially since we had the boys along. I didn't mention my secret relief that we would break up the fifteen miles over two days. Even this first leg of the trip had me ready to chew aspirin.

We found a good spot on the shoulders of the bald near a clutch of small trees that would give us somewhere to string a laundry line. Because I'd spared no luxury, I pulled out a pair of pajama bottoms and a sweatshirt and hung up my sweaty hiking clothes to dry. While the boys collected sticks of firewood, I tinkered with what kindling we already had at hand while Mark broached the wine bag. Once I had a steady chain of smoke puttering, I stuck my canteen cup under the nozzle and filled it to the rim. After a few sips, the memory of trail aches began to fade, as did my interest in maintaining a weak flame. We decided the firelight would only interfere with our stargazing anyhow and resigned ourselves to puffer jackets and watch caps once the sun slipped beyond the mountains.

That night was as clear as we'd hoped. After the brilliant sunset, the world revealed its true immensity. All that glowing distance made visible. We watched shooting stars and satellites and talked about many similar nights we'd enjoyed like this one. The boys sat with us for a while, but they didn't have the built-in capacity for sentimentalism Mark and I did. They went to the tents and listened to us talk while they flipped through books they'd packed in. I remembered what it was like to stay up and listen to adults at camp, often telling stories or lies or some marriage of the two. It was a window into what to expect from adult life, I thought at the time, though like anyone who's ever dwelt on their future, I saw only the parts that I wanted to see, bending the pieces into agreeable shapes. The easy laughter and the sense of stories in your background that were worth telling. The stoic acceptance of whatever natural obstacle was beyond your control. This was how real men behaved, I told myself. Of course, my problem was obvious. I had been, and still was, a romantic.

Perhaps that same desire to root out the best elements of things was what drew me to outdoor excursions with Iain. Though it's a sentiment often phrased with no small degree of irony, I do still believe in the significance of so-called male bonding. On rivers and lakes and in the woods, I've had an unusually rich experience of friendship. I believe some of the best times Ethan and I spent together were rafting the Chattooga River, and I suppose it's impossible to not want to repeat the essence of that with Iain, though he is a different child and I have become a far different parent.

We finished our wine and decided to turn in. By the time I crawled inside my sleeping bag the weather had begun to cool but the moon cast a soft glow over the fly. Perfect sleeping weather, my grandfather would have called it. Maybe so, but it was hard to shut my eyes with the thought of the magnitude overhead. It's the closest thing I believe we can come to blasphemy. Not being awed by the extreme luck of being able to contemplate such a wonder.

I KNEW a storm had moved in when I opened my eyes sometime in the middle of the night to the sound of the tent walls beating against my face. As my sight adjusted, I saw the doorway flail directly overhead. Everything had come unstrung. The stakes had come up and at least one of the poles had collapsed. Pellets of rain lashed everything in camp. You could hear the sick pock as the downpour struck brimming puddles.

"You awake?" I asked.

Iain stirred like the half-drowned creature that he was.

"Yeah," he said. "There's a lot of water over here on this side."

The nonpaternal thought crossed my mind that better over there than over here. Along with the rain, the temperature had dropped dramatically, was now likely in the low forties. The wind gusts had to have been close to fifty miles an hour, perhaps more.

"This isn't good."

"No," I agreed. "It most definitely is not."

Having nothing that could be done until first light, we burrowed back into our sleeping bags and tried to wait things out. Several hours later I could hear rustling and rumbling from Mark and Silas's tent.

"You all wet over there?" Mark wanted to know.

"We've gone amphibious."

"Yeah, us too."

We shouted like that back and forth for a while, no one curious enough about what it looked like outside to actually hazard a look. I scrounged around in my pack for energy bars and beef jerky. We didn't bother heating water for coffee. After a cheerless breakfast, we wrestled our way out of the defeated tent. What had been a monumental overlook the night before was a solid wall of chilling fog driven by gale force winds. It was then that I realized all of my hiking clothes had been left out on the line. They were as wet as if they'd been dragged up from the bottom of a lake. A rookie mistake if there had ever been one. We didn't have time to self-flagellate, though. I wrung everything out and stuffed it in my ruck, told Iain to start striking camp. He didn't need any encouragement. The weather was taskmaster enough on its own.

Ten minutes later we were ready to step off so that we could at least get off the bald and hope for better shelter down on the main trail. I zipped up my Patagonia jacket as far up the neck as it would go and snugged on my watch cap. The only problem was my pants. My only reasonably dry bottoms were my pajamas, which were a harlequin pattern of blue and black checks. I literally looked like the fool I was.

A few minutes on the trail and I was glad to be clear of the higher elevation, regardless of my outfit. The Alabama songwriter Jason Isbell counsels southern men not to ever call what they wear an outfit, but if he could have laid eyes on me in that moment, I imagine he would have had to conceded that as a passably accurate description. It was also good to be on a downhill grade, the weight on my shoulders propelling me forward, though I was still slow enough that I was bringing up the rear.

I was happy to see Iain moving forward at a brisk pace. He and Silas put some distance between themselves and Mark and me. Despite a three-year age difference, they chatted companionably and seemed to get along awfully well. I knew that age differences between boys could be hard. April and I had seen it with Ethan and Iain when we blended the family. Blended was the right word too. Chopped and grinded a bit too. Almost as soon as April and I married, I could see the poorly buried resentment Ethan had for his younger stepbrother. In a letter written to me years later, and which I've only been able to read once after he died, Ethan talked about his rage at having to come to terms with the boy who was the same age that he was when I'd moved away to finish graduate school. He wrote about how he felt he had been replaced and had no say about the damage that would do to our relationship. He said that like many other times in his life, he felt like I had put a woman before him. If he were standing in front of me now, I could not deny that he was right.

Around midday we came to the Overmountain Shelter, a barnlike edifice marking the historical passage of a band of Revolutionary guerillas on their way to whip the British at the Battle of King's Mountain. There was a watering hole down there and we'd all run close to dry. After grounding packs with Iain posted as guard, we went down to fill our bottles straight from the stream. Mark had told us that we were about to get into the climb and that we would need as much water as we could carry.

I watched Silas and Mark working shoulder to shoulder. It was a routine that looked natural, though I knew how much emotional work must have remained hidden beneath the surface. The illusion of ease that results only after years of rigorous method. I've admired Mark's ability to parent over the years and wanted to have the patience and insight that appears to be intuitive in him, though I suspect that it's far more likely a result of focus and discipline. I've tried to learn from it, but I've fallen short more times than not. I recognize now that there was a brief period, perhaps only a few months, where Iain and I had turned a corner, that we had settled into something beyond mere function, that real, demonstrated affection was possible. But when Ethan died, each kindness I gave to Iain seemed like a betrayal, and many of the open doors between us abruptly slammed shut. In the years since, we've each been trying to pry those places free.

By the time we'd charged our water bottles, the wind had blown in another solid bank of wet fog; the trees groaned as they flexed and bent. Even in jackets and watch caps, we still suffered from the chill. I was not excited about the prospect of line drying my soaked gear once we got to a place that would support a second night's camp. With little need for persuasion, we decided it would be best to go ahead and hike all the way out, spend a dry night indoors. The boys seemed pleased with this change of plans. A little electric thrill rippled through us as we rejoined the trail.

Almost immediately, though, I began to fall behind. Much of the morning had been flat or on a gentle downhill grade, but here we began to climb again. The weight on my back was a pain so immediate that it seemed personalized, as if it were a curse devised for insult to my own specific shortcomings. Every dozen yards or so, I would cinch down on the straps and try to heave the pack to some better center of gravity that simply did not exist. The boys had already disappeared up around the distant bend, and even Mark was having a hard time hanging back at such a pace. I told him to go on, I'd get there in my own time.

I caught up with them at the base of Hump Mountain where we sheltered for half an hour in the lee of boulders. If the wind could be said to sing, then it was broken and tuneless. We couldn't hear one another above the roar of it, so we made ourselves small against the rocks, pulled up our jackets into makeshift hoods. This was supposed to be the grand overlook of the whole hike. Instead, the whole way up was smothered in gray. All I could imagine was miserable distance. At a certain point, the delay became worse than the conditions, and we shuffled back on the trail and began the climb. Once more, I fell back.

It's no secret that physical discomfort drives you deep

into yourself. Nothing is more personal than pain. Long-distance runners and elite mountain climbers probably know this far better than most of us. But regardless of your level of training or ability, I believe that battling with your limitations is a good way to understand what is true and what is illusory about your self-concept. Even as I progressed with maddening slowness, I knew I could finish the hike, had no choice really. What I didn't realize until then was how emotional being on the trail with Iain was. It would be hard to explain the sense of loss I felt as I saw him draw far ahead and become lost in the fog. It was a success to see him do well, to see him grow stronger and more confident in himself. But even those successes couldn't help but call up those past inadequacies as a stepfather and father. That's what parenting has seemed to be in the years I've tried my hand at it—a long sequence of things I should have handled better.

Later that day, we would make the peak of the mountain and then descend below the storm line. Plenty of sun and dry ground, but that close to the end, we decided to go on. With the advantage of better weather, it was easy to believe that it hadn't been as bad as it seemed at the time. Again, that trick of the mind. The memory of pain is only a shadow of what it actually was. But that's exactly what I rely on. Only an amnesiac is fool enough to keep trying.

The next summer Iain and I brought his mother to do the same hike. She had heard us talk about it and wanted to see what he and I had been up to together. Half an hour on the trail and the storm clouds honored their afternoon threat. As we climbed toward camp that first evening, we didn't follow a trail. We waded upstream. Everything we had was soaked. My wife didn't believe me when I said I knew where we were going, but Iain assured her that we did. He stopped and held out his hand to help her across a ledge of slippery rock. I saw her take his hand with complete trust, and I thought for a moment that's what I hope it is like when he is left here in the world to care for her after I've crossed over to weightless irrelevance.

A Year
without Months

——

FOR A long time after Ethan died, it was as though the seasons had stopped. Just time coming in a heavy, heavy slide. We lived then, and still do, in a stone cottage. It was good to be surrounded by all that rock, as if the magnitude of geologic time could shelter us from the shattered chronology of each successive day.

The phone call came from the Asheville Police Department on a Friday evening. It was the day before Halloween, and we so enjoyed the early cool spell that we had laid our first fire of the fall. A fire in the fireplace is always a celebration because it conjures up the nostalgic past. I remember once my uncle had explained that combustion was the release of the solar energy that had grown the trees we burned. Even now when I burn wood it feels like sunlight is released inside our home.

It was a woman's voice on the other end of the telephone. I suppose she was a specialist in what she did, delivering messages of death. I remember she used the word *deceased*. It's a particular word, beautiful even. As though the entanglement of life is somehow made elegant by the finality of its close. To cease, to stop. To mercifully end the race that can only conclude with absence and sorrow.

HIS GRANDFATHER, my former father-in-law, had him cremated. Like a kindly Solomon, Frank had half the remains shipped to Ethan's mother and the other half to me. I had been contacted and asked if I wanted to view the body beforehand, but I had said that I didn't want to see him like that.

The summer before, he had grown tall and developed broad shoulders. I remember being struck by how he had the body of a man now as I watched him swim in the lee of a boulder in the Chattooga River, and I was proud to see that this was who he had become. We had beached the raft to delay our arrival at the second night's camp. Though the water was low that year, we still had plenty of afternoon sun and were in no hurry to get off the river, so the six of us had dragged both our boats up on the South Carolina bank while those in kayaks scouted ahead. Everyone else was sprawled on the sand watching the sky to see if we could spot birds of prey. But Ethan was more at home in the river, so he swam, tested himself and his new strength against the current.

It was our third trip on the Chattooga and had become something we looked forward to each year. My friend, Mark, and his brothers, Cliff and James, had been making the run for the better part of two decades. But this annual June trip had swelled, and now it attracted a dozen or more paddlers, drawn by the agreeable company and the chance to camp for a couple of nights along the famed stretch of water. For the two of us, the river gave a chance to escape some of the weight fathers and sons can unwittingly shoulder, and we were happy to have that reprieve, even if it lasted for such a short period of time.

The six months before the Chattooga camp had been un-usually hard. In January, just two months shy of his eigh-teenth birthday, Ethan left in the middle of the night after I'd confronted him about smoking pot in the house, a habit of his which had become increasingly flagrant. It came after two years of living exclusively with his stepmom, April, and me. Much of the time had been difficult, as anyone who has endured the particular demands of a blended family knows, but there had been plenty of good that had come out of it too. I was dazed when I found his room empty the next morning. I spent much of that morning and early afternoon simply driving around town. I suppose if someone would have asked what I was hoping to find, I would have said that I was looking for him, but I knew there was no real chance of doing so. Instead, I was more like a dog suffering some hurt it doesn't understand. I needed to circle and circle before exhaustion made me settle into accepting this injury that was now part of me.

It was a couple of weeks before word got back that he had rented an apartment a few minutes up the road. His source of income for such a move was troubling. What he earned working part-time in the kitchen of a pizza place certainly couldn't explain things. We suspected drug dealing of some kind but had no hard proof. Despite our fears that he was becoming involved in something that could easily get away from him, we were glad we had him geographi-cally fixed.

Now, a few months later, just when we thought that we'd turned a corner and he had a country of promise before him, he was inside a cardboard container the size of a candy box. I sat in the sunroom with the hard autumn light coming through the glass, stared at my books and cluttered desk while the hours overtook me. Sometimes, I glanced at the box. If friends came to visit me, I'm certain they were relieved by how well I seemed to be holding up. How else could I act? It was merely the beginning of what is a lifelong sentence.

A COUPLE of weeks after he died, April and I drove to the apartment building where his car had been left in the corner of the packed dirt parking lot. April had come with Iain a couple of times to check up on him after he left our house. I kept my distance from his place. I didn't want him to feel threatened. I didn't want him to simply disappear. It seemed to have worked. He began to meet us for the occasional lunch, and later we began to make plans for him to move to Knoxville and stay in the spare bedroom while he got on his feet. We even discussed enrolling at the community college where I teach. He updated his Facebook page to reflect that he was a future student at Pellissippi State. The evening we received the call from the police was the day before he was supposed to drive his few things down to Tennessee and move in.

It was already dark by the time we got to the apartment complex. There wasn't much in the way of streetlights, so we each took a flashlight and began to rummage through his effects. His best friend Jake had already gathered boxes of things from inside the apartment, so we were spared from having to cross that threshold. Instead, we rummaged through the T-shirts, scrap papers, and orphaned charging cords, every imaginable aspect of an uncatalogued life. After a few minutes, I noticed a man standing in the open doorway of the facing apartment unit. Backlit as he was, it was hard to tell his age, but I could see gray highlights in his shoulder length hair. This must have been Edward, the hippie neighbor who had told Jake he would watch the car until we could come by and see what was left there we might want to take back home. I knew that I should go over and introduce myself. When I said who I was, he nodded and lit a cigarette. Behind him on his kitchen shelves, I could see row after row of empty liquor bottles with candles stuck in their necks, the festive colors of old candlewax spidering down the glass.

He told me that he'd seen Ethan the day before he died. They often had bonfires in the far corner of the lot. It was that kind of place, he said, where everyone looked after one another. He asked me if we were going to take the car, and I told him that his mother said she wanted it. Said it meant something to her, though I imagine she needed the vehicle for practical reasons. I was certainly in no mood to fight her for it. But it should be gone soon. For some reason, I felt the need to put the man at ease about something that didn't concern him.

"There's something else that the police let me have, if you want it."

He told me to wait while he got it from his bedroom. While he was gone, I watched April carrying more garbage bags of dirty clothes from Ethan's car to ours. We were almost done. We could drive back and sort everything out there. All I wanted was to be sealed up in our home, away from this place that held eeriness and regret.

When Edward came back, he handed me the small pull-up bar. I remember Ethan clamping it to his bedroom door frame at our Candler house before April, Iain, and I moved to Knoxville for my teaching job. On the middle of the bar was a tight leather knot with a frayed edge. I recognized it to be the bitter end of one of my old belts I'd given to Ethan.

"They had to cut him down," Edward told me. "I don't know what they did with the rest of it."

I asked him to tell me what else the police had said. I wanted to know every possible detail.

"It was in the back closet," he said. "And he had a bag over his head to make sure it took. Didn't want to risk surviving with brain damage, I guess."

For some reason, I thanked him before I left.

I KEPT the pull-up bar in the sunroom where I sat for several weeks. It's strange how something that may seem a grisly reminder to an outsider can be a comfort to those who are most directly touched by the object. The material presence made the room cohere. It gave me something tangible to mourn.

For a while there, I allowed myself to become obsessed with the mystery of Ethan's act. I approached it from every possible angle. There was no note left before he hanged himself, though the leaving of a note is more often in film and drama than it is in the real world. Still, his silence invited speculation. I wanted to know as much as I could. But he was evasive even in death. His laptop history had been erased, his email accounts deleted. All we had were the few conversations with some of his friends he'd called in the days leading up to his death. When I asked one of them if they had any idea why he did it, he shrugged and said only, "He was good at keeping secrets."

The secrets are what kept us apart. At times, when we would fight and he would come to the point of teary frustration, he seemed almost at the point of disclosing something, but at the last moment he would always pull back. I told him that he could tell me whatever he needed to, but he refused, saying that he couldn't trust me. Eventually, he agreed to see a counselor, as long as I promised that I would let whatever he said with her remain confidential. I agreed.

We saw Colleen for the next couple of months. She specialized in younger children mostly, but sometimes counseled teens as well. Her practice was in a partitioned Victorian kept warmly hospitable with ticking radiators and well-worn club chairs. At the back was a large kitchen where parents could pour themselves a cup of coffee and wait out as best they could while their kids poured out the messy parts of being human upstairs.

It was hard to say if it helped much. He allowed her to give me general feedback on how the sessions went. She said that he was often tired and didn't talk freely. What was certain, she said, was that he suffered from posttraumatic stress, though the details of what that may have been remained between her and him.

I DREAM often of my grandmother, though she's been dead for more than twenty years. In the dreams she feels immediate in a way that the rest of my family, all dead now, does not. There isn't much to these meetings. They are truly just visitations, though the presence is something so palpable that when I wake I find that I'm actually weeping in my sleep, and when I sit up in bed it takes a few minutes to rid myself of the intense reality of her death.

I have a photograph of her taken when Ethan when he was only a few weeks old. She is in a wheelchair and he is perched in her lap, a decidedly nervous glint in his eyes. She would die a little over a year later, so I know he had no memory of her, but I like that this was documented, their single meeting. I had received special leave from the Marine Corps to travel home so that she would have this chance. My mother is also in the frame of the photograph, though I often forget that detail. She and I could never fully repair our relationship after I met Ethan's mother. Jealousy and resentment became as clear with her as if it had been written on her skin. Because of that, her love had become conditional, qualified. In many ways, she had long ceded the role of mother to my grandmother. Perhaps that's why my memory for detail is so selective when I remember what it was like to bring my son back home, to show the promise he held.

Strangely, I never dream of Ethan.

IT CAN be a terrible seduction to think more about the dead than the living. In death, I found, Ethan surpassed me. He was the one with the completed story, the one who had seen things through to the end. There's a kind of admiration to be found in that, though that's a dangerous line of thought to pursue too far.

I've always thought that Hamlet gets it wrong when he claims that the death of his father sends "time out of joint." It's exactly the opposite. Just as Claudius counsels him, the death of the parent is the greatest fidelity time can possess. The loss belongs to an order than we've prepared for our whole lives. With lost children, though, the order is broken apart and reassembled. The past tense carries unassailable authority. The dead, regardless of their age, father us all.

I RETURNED to teaching less than a week after his death. It was the only way I knew to move forward. The regular repetition of class meetings and reading schedules offered a pattern I could pin my life to. I realize now that my commitment to this was so complete that I have little sense of the details. I walked around, somehow talked and seemed to listen when others spoke, though I was more personality than person for a long time. An automation. Anything could bring on a panic. A song on the radio, a shift in the afternoon light. Once, while I sat in a car line to pick up Iain from middle school, the wind tossed the boughs of neighborhood trees in such a way that I began to weep uncontrollably.

The sharpest sense I felt when I thought of him was absence. I didn't then and still don't have much of what could be rightly called any religious feeling about what happened to Ethan after he was gone. Those beliefs have always seemed to trivialize the dead to my mind. I've read that many parents of suicides go through periods of anger, but this was never the case with me. I was only curious what it must have been like for him in those small hours leading up to the decision. What were the small comforts he managed in the last deliberate actions he took? In contemplating this, I felt a kind of connection, though why I found it so is still largely inexpressible.

I RESEARCHED suicide on the Internet. At first I checked statistics, but soon I started looking for other things like how to do it, and especially how to do it well. What an odd convenience to have at hand. I wasn't looking into it for my own benefit, though that again is common with surviving parents. Instead, I wanted to walk through the steps Ethan had, to reify the abstraction. My father and uncle had found their commitment at the bottom of a bottle, but I suspect it was different for Ethan. He had devised his fate with intelligence and skill. The details I'd learned that night at the apartment complex made that clear.

Though I couldn't be certain that he had found the same information I did, it seemed likely. A young man had put up a site detailing step-by-step the most effective means of killing yourself by hanging. Of course, he appended the entire prospectus with a note that there were reasons to resist the desire to end your life. I remember that he even included a hyperlink to a suicide prevention page. And while the candor of the website was bracing, there was a degree of real empathy in what had been written as well. It was clear that the author wanted to spare the reader any unnecessary physical suffering. He wanted the hurting to be no worse than it had to be.

Shortly before Ethan moved out of his mother's house to live full time with me, he expressed an interest in Judo. He knew I had practiced with my uncle for several years when I was a boy. It seemed like a good thing for us to do together, and there was a club that met not far from downtown where we could go and practice together. I ordered uniforms for us, and we began to attend twice a week.

Unlike karate, Judo avoids striking moves in favor of wrestling-like takedowns and grappling maneuvers. Though it is usually high impact, the fighting is done on thick mats that absorb the brunt of physical shock. So, despite the violent appearance, the hand-to-hand combat is largely safe, with the occasional contusions, sprains, and joint injuries you might find in most contact sports. Ethan seemed to take to it naturally. I think, too, he enjoyed the chance to get out on the mat and square off with me. He would often reserve special aggression for our bouts, though that isn't necessarily an advantage in a discipline that prizes balance.

One of the parts of Judo that can intimidate new fighters the most is when the fighting goes to the ground. This is called mat work, and it involves wrestling moves, arm bars, and choking. Many people panic when they feel the crush of another body on top of them and will tap out from the pressure of the hold, claustrophobia overthrowing them far easier than a truly dominant position can. One of the keys to getting used to this feeling is the ability to calm yourself and make space by wiggling out a knee or elbow, even if your opponent has the upper hand. Once a fighter understands that they can breathe, the real chess match of bodies can begin.

The counterpoint against this, however, is the deadly suddenness of the Judo choke. Unlike what is often seen in film, this attack doesn't seize the windpipe, which could cause serious injury but takes much longer to subdue your opponent. Instead, the Judo choke targets the blood flow to the brain. If the hold is accurately applied, the victim will experience a few seconds of giddy lightheadedness before essentially falling asleep. There is no prolonged suffering.

The fact that Ethan understood how to do this has lent me great comfort.

WHILE IT remains true that religion has failed to console me, there was one time I felt that I was with Ethan after his death. The summer after he was gone, I went with students on a study abroad to Japan. One weekend, while the students were exploring on their own, I went down to Kamakura, an hour south of Tokyo. The city is popular for its history, the seaside, and the Kotoku-in, the eight-hundred-year-old towering Buddha cast in bronze. But there's another site a few minutes' walk from the train station, the Hase-dera, a temple dedicated to the bodhisattva Kannon, that drew my attention.

Like so many temples in Japan, the temple grounds were exquisitely groomed. The shrines and statues were lovely. And the great attraction, the thirty-foot tall wooden carving of Kannon herself with her elaborately detailed

eleven heads, each turned toward a different aspect of en-
lightenment, was quietly overwhelming. But what pulled me
most was the cave system beneath the temple. Despite the
heat of the day, the caves were cool and dripped down to
standing pools that rose to the edges of the paving stones.
I followed the winding circle that faced a series of candlelit
statues. Here, I learned, was a depiction not of Kannon,
but of Benzaiten, another female bodhisattva, but who was
also a Shinto deity of the sea. As I continued, the passage
lowered so that I had to deeply stoop to go on before
another chamber and passage revealed itself. To the right, I
saw another small grotto which was filled with hundreds of
small wooden Buddhas. Amid them, like small lampposts,
dozens of candles burned. I saw a small offering box next to
another container of Buddhas and several magic markers. It
took me a few moments to realize that these were prayers
of a kind. I placed a hundred-yen coin in the box and wrote
Ethan's name on the base of one of the wooden Buddhas,
settled it among the other remembrances people had left in
the cave. It seemed right that it was a ritual I could only
partly understand.

WHEN ETHAN was still only two, I awakened to tumbling
dark and an odd swelling of nausea. His mother realized
what was happening before I did and ran for his bedroom. I
remained in bed, staring stupidly at the ceiling as the house
heaved like it was a ship at sea. By the time I was able to
get to my feet and follow her, the earthquake had begun to
subside.

   In his bedroom I found her standing over him; he had
slept through what we would later learn was a 7.1 earthquake with an epicenter about a dozen miles from our front
door. I tried to make a joke about it, but even as dazed as I

was, I was ashamed that I hadn't reacted quicker. I should have been there. Intuition should have driven me. Instead, I'd been paralyzed with disorientation. Only luck had spared us a collapsed ceiling or fractured wall.

I went to the window facing away from the base housing neighborhood and out into the desert darkness. It was somehow more immense by the disturbance of the earthquake. I tried the hallway light switch, but the power was out. I told his mother I was going down to the car to turn on the radio to see if I could get any details. But when I got the car started and went through the local stations, only static came through. Outside, the eerie solitude was so total that I walked around for a while, gazing on the silent dark, as if trying to register something like that as completely as I could.

The first sound was the yipping of coyotes. At first only a few, but then many. Building to a full pitch. It was as terrible and lovely as anything I'd ever heard. They were making sure their kin was still safe out there in the night.

I STILL haven't managed to give up Ethan's ashes. No one has pressured me to, but it seems like something I need to come to terms with at some point. In the years since he's been gone, I've considered different places he loved. The Chattooga River is one of the first that comes to mind. In one of his final social media posts, he uploaded a picture of a kayak beached on a small island. He had taken it on our final trip down the river together. Below the photograph, he mentioned that the river was one of the places that made him feel most human.

There's also an area he called "The Cut," an overlook of Asheville where he used to go with his friends after sunset and look over the city. Likely they smoked and drank illicitly and had youthful conversations about the life they imagined stretched out before them. He would probably like that, the chance to be commemorated as what he was. A young man with promise.

But burials are more for the living than the dead. Because we're still here, we get to decide. And I want him to rest where I can visit him regardless of whether life picks us up from where we are. I want him to have a simple stone in the woods in a pleasant glade. I want the wind to always blow. I think he'll like the way the tossing of tree boughs sounds like gossip.

When I'm ready, I'll take him there. I don't know yet if I'll need to do it alone.

IT'S COMMONLY held that the death of a child is hardest on the mother. Perhaps, but there's this:

A week after Ethan was born, his mother and I took him to the pediatrician at the navy hospital for his first health and wellness check. Almost as soon as he saw Ethan, he became alarmed.

"This isn't right. He's dehydrated."

He ran the vitals, began to place urgent calls to nurses in the office. The phrase "failure to thrive" was repeated like a hammer stroke. He needed to be medevacked to Balboa Hospital in San Diego immediately. If not, they told us, he could be dead within hours. We watched him go out the door in a special travel-ready incubator on his way to the helicopter. When they placed the IV into his listless arm, his mother began to cry. I pulled her away so that we could drive the three hours to the intensive care unit where they were flying him.

Once there, he was kept warm under a special heat lamp. We sat by and watched as the doctors and nurses cared for him. Days went by like that. Sleep evaded us until it would grab hold with inescapable gravity, and when we would wake time would have come uncoupled. Even now, I can't recall exactly how long we were trapped in that peculiar dread. A week, at least. Perhaps two.

What I remember best is how he had to be fed. He was too weak to try to breastfeed, but they encouraged his mother to pump milk. We had two options. We could transition to bottle feeding, or we could try something that the nurses said made it more likely that he could eventually return to nursing from his mother. A small tube was run from a bottle of breast milk and taped to the pinky finger. As the milk dripped down, the baby could latch to the finger and use it as a substitute nipple. Because the source of the milk was flesh, the child would trust the sense and smell, keep its faith by the blood bond. I asked if it mattered whether it was the mother or the father that gave the baby milk. Any human hand would do, they said.

Today, despite the fractured memories, I can remember those days with him in my arms, how he weighed with the heavy years to come. Years that he would endure as we failed him and he failed himself. But I am still thrilled by that powerful drive he had to drink in the milk and proud too of his spirit as he fought his way into the world with the comfort of my hand.

Acknowledgments

—

My gratitude and thanks to Derek Krissoff at West Virginia University Press, for his early support and enthusiasm for this book; to Jeremy Jones and Elena Passarello, for their stewardship of the In Place series; Anne McPeak, for her expert eye and voice; and Sara Georgi, for her kindly shepherding. As before, this book exists because of A., E., and I.